Chi

D0366713

How to Write Romances

REVISED AND UPDATED

HOW TO WRITE ROMANCES

PHYLLIS TAYLOR PIANKA

WRITER'S DIGEST BOOKS
CINCINNATI, OHIO

02 01 00 99 98 5 4 3 2 1

Library of Congress Cataloging-in-Publication Data

Pianka, Phyllis Taylor.
  How to write romances / by Phyllis Taylor Pianka.—Rev. and updated.
      p.   cm.
  Includes bibliographical references and index.
  ISBN 0-89879-867-1
  1. Love stories—Authorship. 2. Creative writing. I. Title.
PN3377.5.L68P54   1998
808.3′85—dc21   98-23353
                                                            CIP

Edited by David Borcherding
Production edited by Michelle Howry
Cover designed by Brian Roeth

Acknowledgments

With sincere appreciation to those who have contributed their expertise to the success of this book and to those authors whose book I have reviewed.

Ethan Ellenberg, Ethan Ellenberg Literary Agency. Shauna Summers, Editor, Ballantine Publishing Group. Louise Snead, Publisher, *Affaire de Coeur*. Kathryn Falk, Publisher, *Romantic Times*. Jan Mussell, Bookseller. Debra Mekler, writer/President SVRWA.

And the following authors: Francine Rivers, Kathryn Makris, Nora Roberts, Lindsay Longford, Trisha Alexander, Irma Ruth Walker, Jayne Ann Krentz, Elizabeth Lowell, Kim Lewis, Johanna Lindsey, Suzanne Brockmann, and many other talented authors whose work I have mentioned. A few of them are:

Candice Hern. *A Garden Folly* ©1997 and *An Affair of Honor*, Signet Regency Romance/Penguin Books. All rights reserved

Kate Hoffman. *The Honeymoon Deal* ©1997 Harlequin Temptation®/Harlequin® Enterprises Limited All rights reserved.

Joanna Wayne. *Family Ties* ©1997 Harlequin Intrigue®/Harlequin® Enterprises Limited. All rights reserved.

Alexandra Sellers. *Bride of The Sheikh* ©1997 Silhouette Intimate Moments®/Sihouette® Books. All rights reserved.

Rosalyn Alsobrook. *For The Love Of Pete* ©1997 Seascape Romance/Contemporary Romance/St. Martin's Press. All rights reserved.

Susan Plunkett. *Silver Tomorrows* ©1997 Jove and *Heaven's Time* © 1998 Time Passages Historical Novel. The Berkley Publishing Group. All rights reserved.

Dorothy Garlock. *Larkspur* ©1997 Historical Novel/Warner Books. All rights reserved.

Kate Kingsley. *The Scout's Bride* ©1997 Harlequin® Historical/Harlequin® Enterprises Limited. All rights reserved.

Diana Whitney. *A Hero's Child* ©1997 Sihouette Special Edition®/Silhouette® Books. All rights reserved.

And especially to Michelle Howry, Production Editor at Writer's Digest Books.

About the Author

Writing in both contemporary and historical romance categories, best-selling author Phyllis Taylor Pianka has sold twenty novels. They have been translated into twenty-two languages, recorded for the blind and reprinted in large type for the sight impaired. Her publishers include Dell, Jove and Harlequin. A prize-winning author of short stories and articles for national magazines, she was also a newspaper correspondent for two years and is well-known for her seven how-to booklets for writers.

Some of her novels include a trio of Regency novels from Harlequin: *The Calico Countess*, *The Lark's Nest* and *The Coventry Courtship*. Under her pseudonym, Winter Ames, Berkley/Jove released the contemporary novels *Emerald Bay* and *Bird of Paradise*. Her most recent novel is a six-hundred-page Regency trilogy, *The Thackery Jewels*, from Harlequin. She is currently at work on another Regency and a contemporary women's novel.

As a public speaker in the field of creative writing, Pianka has lectured at dozens of colleges and universities throughout the country. She is a frequent speaker at the national conferences of Romance Writers of America and is a staff lecturer for The Writer's Connection and the Celebrity Speakers Bureau. Pianka teaches extension courses at the University of California at Berkeley, as well as a ten-week on-line course entitled "Introduction to Fiction."

Pianka is founder of Cupertino Writers, cofounder of Bay Area Chapter of Romance Writers of America and a charter member of Romance Writers of America. Other memberships include: San Francisco Bay Chapter/RWA, Silicon Valley Chapter/RWA, Published Authors' Network (PAN), California Writers' Club and The Writer's Connection.

Contents

Introduction
About This Book

Writing a romance novel is one of the best ways for a novice writer to achieve publication.

Once looked down upon as morally corrupting, romance novels now comprise 53 percent of mass market sales and are the mainstay of many publishers of book-length popular fiction.

The average reader of romance novels spends up to thirty dollars per month on books. Some 40 percent are college educated, 35 percent are employed full time, 20 percent read one romance a day and 40 percent read one romance novel every two days. Although these books are read mainly by women, many men now admit they enjoy not only reading romance novels but writing them as well.

Except for a number of writers you know well, romance novelists are unlikely to become rich, but they can earn a surprising income. Prolific authors, such as Janet Dailey, Patricia Matthews, Elizabeth Lowell, Nora Roberts, Jayne Ann Krentz and LaVyrle Spencer who have grown from comparative obscurity to international popularity in a few short years, do very well indeed.

Publishers have pulled back from the huge advances they once offered romance novelists. Advances now run anywhere from five hundred to several thousand dollars, but the average advance for a first novel is about five thousand dollars.

It isn't necessary to know an editor to have your book published. Many authors, including me, sold their first romance novel over the transom—a term denoting an unsolicited novel sent directly to the publisher without benefit of a literary agent. I began writing in my early forties, through an adult education class taught by Helene Schellenberg Barnhart. In this class I learned the basics of manuscript submission and how to select a market. A month after I began, I sold my first short story for eleven dollars.

After that I wrote several articles and became a correspondent for a local newspaper, but I soon found that fiction was more fun and more profitable.

My first novel, a Gothic, was rejected because the publisher was no longer printing the genre. The editor liked my style, however, and asked me to write a one-page proposal for a nurse novel. I did. It sold, and so did the next novel I wrote for that company.

Time and experience taught me there was a more businesslike way to sell a manuscript. I enlisted the services of a literary agent and earned over two thousand dollars more on my next contracted novel (a contemporary romance for Dell) than on my first two novels. And when Regency novels became popular, my agent sold my first Regency novel as well as several contemporary romances.

It sounds easy, doesn't it? Still, writing and selling are both easier and harder than I expected. I believed that once you had a few books published, you'd never have to worry about rejections. You do. The publishing business is ever changing, and a writer must never forget that being a writer is being a professional student. You must never stop learning.

Writing is a business, and you must learn the ground rules as in any other business. You must study the markets to understand how each publisher's demands differ from the others and then select a story line that meets those demands and also contains fresh and original elements. Finally, you must create vibrant and sympathetic characters with whom your readers can identify.

This book is for the beginning writer who would like to write romance fiction, and for the advanced writer who would like to break into the romance field or simply improve his or her writing skills. These writing skills apply not only to romance fiction but to fiction in general. *How to Write Romances* is a step-by-step guide, beginning with the search for an idea and leading to the selling of your manuscript to a publisher.

Most publishers of romance series offer a set of guidelines. These tip sheets provide the publishers' specifications for the basic structure of their romance novels, but they cannot dictate the writer's interpretation of those guidelines—the creative process through which a writer takes the guidelines and writes hundreds of different plots. Here is where the real excitement begins. It's like learning to walk. Once you've mastered the basics, you can go as far as you wish.

There is no journey more exciting, more rewarding, than your own fantasy trip with characters and settings spun from the fabric of your own imagination.

1

Before You Begin to Write

Series Novels vs. Single Titles
Series Novels

Genre, or series novels are novels usually produced as a line, with a given number of new books in that line published each month. They must appeal to a select group of readers, and are a common fixture of genre fiction. Some examples are romances, westerns, science fiction, action/adventures and mysteries (many of these categories also have subcategories). Series novels are usually small books, running 55,000 words to 85,000 words in length.

Unlike some mainstream novels, series novels are not meant to propagandize or to sway a reader's opinion. Series novels are written to entertain. Though they often take place in a different time or a far-off place, romance novels tend to celebrate personal goals, families and commitment . . . not just fun and adventure. Part of the excitement of writing romance is researching careers, locales and time periods to provide authenticity and give the reader something to savor after finishing the book.

Some publishers use the services of book packagers. Book packagers are companies that draw up proposals for a new series or group of books and present the ideas to various publishers. If a publisher decides to purchase the series, he gives the packager a predetermined amount of money to produce the books. The packager then hires authors to write the books, usually to specific guidelines or outlined plots provided by the packager. The author receives a flat fee for this "work for hire" process and, once the book is accepted and the fee paid, the author has no further control over the book. In addition, the author will receive no more money, no matter how well the book sells. Sometimes the author's name appears on the book, but more often a "house name" or pseudonym for a group of authors is used.

Single Titles

Some romances are single title or midlist books—books that stand on their own, rather than being part of a line. A few may qualify as mainstream. Midlist and mainstream novels appeal to a wider range of readers, have fewer restrictions as to content, are distributed more widely and have a longer shelf life than series books. The longer length of these novels, most often 95,000 to 125,000 words, allows the writer to explore characters and situations more fully than in the series novels, which can be as few as 35,000 words. The mainstream novel is more difficult to write and sell.

It is important to understand that single titles and mainstream novels are *not* long series novels. Besides length, another distinction between series and single title novels is that series novels span only a limited amount of time, usually no more than a year. More often, the action takes place in only a few months, except for events in the back story. The story line of mainstream novels can span anywhere from a few hours to generations. Unlike the series romance, which always has a happy ending, mainstream novels may leave situations unresolved, relationships broken or unsatisfactory, and dreams unrealized.

It is fairly easy to see the differences between the series and single title books when you cruise through a bookstore. Series novels are usually shelved in a group. They are thin books shelved according to the line, such as Harlequin Romance, Silhouette Desire and Loveswept. Single title novels are shelved under *Romance*, alphabetically under the author's name. Mainstream novels are shelved as fiction under the author's name, or (for a lucky few) under best-sellers.

A fine line divides single title and mainstream novels. The popularity of a single title or midlist book or that of the author may easily push a novel into mainstream designation.

Many series romance authors have crossed over to single title romance, nonfiction, and mainstream fiction, as well as films, after having learned the basics and having built a track record in series. To name a few: Janet Dailey, Nora Roberts, Elizabeth Lowell (Ann Maxwell), Jayne Ann Krentz (Amanda Quick), Irma Ruth Walker, LaVyrle Spencer and Johanna Lindsey.

Romance Subcategories

Romance falls into several subgenres: Young Adult (*YA novels* as they are called in the industry) with subcategories of YA historical, YA contemporary, and the YA series books with continuing characters (such as the Sweet Valley High series).

Then there are the inspirational romances and Christian romances, both contemporary and historical. Inspirational romance, in particular, is a growth market. The Harlequin Steeple Hill line is expressly devoted to this category. In most of the romance categories mentioned so far, the emphasis is more on the characters than on the romance.

An adult series romance is a story about one woman and one man, who, despite their conflicts, recognize the special chemistry that flows between them, and are able to overcome their differences in order to make a commitment to each other.

Adult series romances can be divided into traditional ("sweet" and comparatively sex-free) romance, and the more sensual romance. Other, more specific, divisions may include time travel, suspense or stories set in specific periods or locations. Publishers' needs differ from year to year, so it is wise to request guidelines from the publisher and read current novels from existing lines.

The romance novel may be set in either the contemporary or historical time period. Historical novels are divided into several additional categories, which we will discuss in chapter eleven.

The romantic intrigue is a fast-paced action story involving intrigue and suspense interwoven into the romantic plot. Several lines now include elements of mystery and intrigue.

The Gothic, another subcategory that can be contemporary or historical, involves the heroine in a mystery that usually threatens her life. The setting is of major importance in creating the suspenseful tone so essential to the Gothic. *Jane Eyre* is a Gothic novel. In today's market, Gothic novels may not be classified as Gothics. They often fall under the category of suspense or simply romance, such as Anne Stuart's Harlequin American Romance, *A Dark & Stormy Night*. You can often rely on book covers to give a clue to the content in this genre.

When addressing the national conference of Romance Writers of America, Christine Zika, an editor from Dell, said that Dell has no series romance lines. They look for contemporary romances of about 100,000 words, approximately 400 double-spaced manuscript pages. "The focus must be on the hero and heroine, but secondary characters may be included," Zika explained. "What we look for is big book quality, with home-based characters. Character-driven stories with psychological angst. The tried-and-true but with a wider canvas and unique twists." She added that they consider paranormal and romantic suspense as well as cross-cultural themes, but at this time they are not looking for "glitz" novels—jet set, Hollywood-type novels of glamour and self-indulgence.

Ethan Ellenberg of the Ethan Ellenberg Literary Agency took time to answer some questions I asked him. He said, "There are a number of things that set apart the published romance novelist from the unpublished. Writing ability is one of them, though don't assume you don't have it until you've worked on a few books. It's definitely something that can surface and be developed.

"Beyond that there are a few things that stand out in my mind. The ability to create truly engaging characters, characters we care for and root for. Great characters can cover or make up for other deficiencies.

"A great story idea that can be translated into a compelling story also tops the list. By this I mean it's not enough to have a great story idea or concept (dinosaurs brought back to life in *Jurassic Park*, for instance). You also have to be able to turn that idea into narrative.

"I read a lot of unpublished writers and my single biggest criticism is that many books I read are simply flat—scenes have little drama or are so overwritten that they could curdle milk. The plotting is aimless and slow, the writing lacking detail and flair.

"I also find some manuscripts haven't really been worked on enough. It's not enough to simply have your hero and heroine and basic story line. Does the story build? Is each scene consistently engaging? If the plotting is flawed, go back and fix it, find a way to make the whole book work. The logical unfolding of the story does matter; don't assume because you have two grand characters you can take excessive liberty with the story.

"I wouldn't want to make any forecasts. I'm consistently amazed by the quality of work that crosses my desk from my client list. I believe romance writing is improving and that more of the top rank of suspense writers will emerge from the romance market. The current environment is difficult, but a lot of people are still building careers and I remain active in my search for talent.

"The best submission to make to me is an outline, the first three sample chapters, a self-addressed stamped envelope for reply and an introductory letter that contains a publishing history or pertinent information."

Getting published is never easy. It takes hard work and dedication whether you are writing for series or mainstream. That fact is one of the few absolutes in this business. Although it may be easier (or, better put, less difficult) to sell a big novel if you already have a track record in the publishing industry, it does not necessarily follow that a bigger book will mean more money for you. Two small books may outearn one large book, but there are many things to take into consideration.

If you dislike reading and writing series romances and intend to use them merely as a stepping-stone to mainstream, you are making a mistake. Editors can spot a phony. Have reverence for the craft.

There are several advantages for authors who are able to write romances. A properly submitted proposal will be read whether it is received over the transom or through an agent. Series novels are short so you don't have to devote a year or more to writing them.

Nora Roberts, author of well over sixty novels, is mentor to countless writers. She says, "The first suggestion [to beginning writers] is always to read, read, read. A writer must understand and enjoy the act of writing, just as he must understand and enjoy the type of writing he's chosen. It's not enough to choose romance writing because you've heard there's money in it. Readers are not fools. Once a writer has developed an affection for romance and an understanding of its purpose, the next step is to write. The RWA [Romance Writers of America] is an invaluable tool for support and information; writing groups and classes always help, but unless a writer has the drive and discipline to sit down and work, day after day, his story won't be told. [When the revisions are complete] find the proper, professional way to submit and mail the manuscript. That's much harder than it sounds. As soon as the manuscript is on its way, start another. It's the best cure for a nervous stomach."

Study the Changing Markets

Many publishers produce one or more romance lines. Some examples are the Harlequin Romance, Harlequin American Romance, Avon

Romance, Silhouette Desire and Silhouette Special Edition.

At present, Harlequin, Silhouette, Zebra and Berkley/Jove represent the major romance publishers. Silhouette was bought by Harlequin but maintains its own imprint.

As is any industry, the publishing business is fluid and cyclical. Authors, whether just beginning or firmly established, must keep informed about the trade, from new lines of romances to changing markets. The best way to do this is to belong to Romance Writers of America, a national organization established by those and for those who work in this field. Also read current editions of *Writer's Market*, which updates the romance trend and markets annually; it's a publication most writers consider the industry's bible. Study recent periodicals such as the RWA's *Romance Writers Report* (RWR) and *Writer's Digest* magazine for marketing information and current needs. It is helpful to belong to an active writer's networking group on the Internet. The help and information available there is astounding. See chapter fourteen on the Internet for more information. You can also refer to the list of references and support groups that appears at the back of this book.

Each publisher and each line within a publishing house has its own editorial slant, enabling a writer to choose the kind of book that most interests her and write to the editor requesting a copy of the current guidelines for that particular romance line. Be sure to enclose a SASE (self-addressed stamped envelope). Guidelines enable a writer to structure or slant the book toward a single line. An unstructured novel can too easily slip between the cracks. If the manuscript is part romance part police procedural novel, it falls between genres and will probably be rejected. The reason? Because the art department does not know what kind of design to put on the cover, and the bookstore owner does not know where to display the book. Readers want to know what kind of book they are buying.

Guidelines provide information such as what kind of heroine and hero the line prefers, what settings are acceptable, the degree of sensuality, the word length, and the preferred manner of submitting a proposal. It is extremely important to use current guidelines.

If there is one piece of advice that editors, lecturers and teachers all agree on, it's the necessity to read voraciously in the field in which you want to write. Read recent releases, first for pleasure, then read and reread to analyze technique and to understand the slant.

Janet Dailey, one of the groundbreakers for romance fiction, is said to have read four hundred Harlequins before she attempted to write one. Her work paid off—there are millions of copies of her books in print.

What Makes a Romance Novel?

Some things are common to all romance novels. Each contains several essential ingredients:

1. A heroine and hero (idealized)
2. A critical situation
3. Conflict
4. Romantic encounters
5. A resolution to the conflict
6. A happy ending in which the hero and heroine make an emotional commitment to each other

Tie these ingredients together with threads of local color, action, immediacy, excitement, humor, pathos and believability, and you have a book that will satisfy and enthrall the reader. Originality counts, but it must be contained within the boundaries set by the editorial guidelines. It is the writer's creativity woven into the fabric of a plot outlined by the tip sheet that can make a book outstanding.

The Changing Markets: Yesterday, Today and Tomorrow

The cycle of the romance novel will continue in one form or another as long as there are readers who want to fall in love, but the form of the romance novel is changing along with the structure of society. Where once the heroine was a Cinderella girl whose only goal was to find a husband (preferably rich) to take care of her and be the father of her children, today's heroine is confident, optimistic, and more mature both in age and outlook. Today's heroine is more independent and reflects modern advantages and concerns; however, she still (almost always) wants a husband and children.

The cycle that began with sweet romance and its virginal heroines has evolved into more sensual stories where the heroine may have had one or two serious emotional involvements. However, she is never promiscuous. As soon as she becomes involved with the hero of the story, she is committed to him despite the conflicts and misunderstandings that must be resolved before they can recognize their commitment.

As readers continue to demand more creativity, romance novels have taken on elements of adventure and increased romantic suspense. The books of Phyllis Whitney and Victoria Holt are among the classics in the genre. Regency and Gothic novels, which were extremely popular for several years, will always be with us. The market is much smaller now for these genres, but there are innovations to keep the categories fresh. The Gothic heroine has matured (some publishers use the term *romantic suspense* instead of *Gothic*) and the Regency heroine is more sensual. Intrigue, adventure, magic and time travel are other trends that have been adopted by various romance lines.

Historical romance novels, with all the subcategories, are so popular that we will devote an entire chapter to their discussion, covering everything from salable ideas to the settings and time periods readers find most compelling.

What are editors looking for? It's not surprising to find that many of them have similar answers.

Leslie Wainger, Senior Editor and Editorial Coordinator for *Intimate Moments* and *Yours Truly* at Silhouette, explained what she likes to see in a submission: "The single most important ingredient is excitement, but that's something deeper and more complicated than it first appears. I don't simply mean action-adventure, though that's certainly a welcome—and effective—aspect of many plots. What I'm talking about is an excitement, even an electricity, to the relationship itself. A book with little conventional action can, in the hands of a master, be the most exciting, simply because the relationship is so involving that I, as the reader, can't resist turning the pages and racing toward the end. It's this compelling quality that all readers respond to and all the best writers weave into their books."

Shauna Summers is a Senior Editor at the Ballantine Publishing Group. "I personally acquire for our list, romances as well as other fiction and nonfiction. We are open to new writers, but we don't have a large list, so we are forced to be extremely selective. In the next year or so, we will be publishing books by two authors who were previously unpublished that I know of—there may be more.

"I couldn't speak to what is most popular right now—that's kind of like trends and I don't believe in them. We are always looking for really fresh, strong voices in all subgenres of romance—a great story with wonderful characters. I know aspiring writers get tired of hearing that, but it's really the truth.

"In general, we don't do much with paranormal—time travel, ghosts, etc.—but that's not to say we wouldn't publish one that we thought was terrific. I do seem to see some more buzz about inspirational romance, but we don't have any immediate plans to acquire in this field. As I already said, I don't believe in trends, and I think writers should write the story that is the fire in their belly, rather than trying to predict or jump on the bandwagon of what they think will sell.

"What excites me most about a new submission is a fresh voice (Do I sound like a broken record?) and good writing. Beyond that, it's kind of hard to describe, but sometimes when I'm reading a submission, I just know—there's that magic there.

"Some common mistakes that writers make in construction of a novel: too much setup and information given all at first or in big chunks, rather than threading the necessary info throughout; Ping-Pong point of view. What I suggest to new writers is to take their favorite books and analyze them very closely. Take them apart and really look at what the author does to develop character, conflict and plot.

"We don't accept unsolicited manuscripts—if a writer doesn't have an agent he or she should send a query letter first with return postage."

Novels are not the only option open to the romance writer. Women's magazines feature condensed novels, or novellas, as well as romantic short stories and contests for writers. The confessions magazine stories are another popular sideline for romance writers. The equivalent of the old ten-cent pulp fiction romances, confession magazines are found under names like *True Story Magazine* and *Modern Romance*. And, of course, once a writer has gained some critical or popular success, there are movies, movies for television, and both audio- and videocassette contracts.

If you are flexible, the research you do for the contemporary and historical romance novel can also pay off through a lecture series or through nonfiction articles written for appropriate periodicals.

What will be popular a few months or years down the road? If we knew, we would all be rich. We can only judge by past experiences and know that each cycle appears to renew itself. Whatever the trend, a book that grabs the reader and holds her so she is unable to put it down is sure to sell eventually.

You *can* learn to write. What it takes is determination, willingness to study the craft, a measure of creativity, and most of all, a love of the genre. Your books will be read by people all over the world, in all walks of life. Best of all, you will have found a career that is like no other. It can open doors for you—doors you never even dreamed existed.

2

Ideas and How to Find Them

Whenever a nonwriter meets an author the question always comes up: "Where do you get your ideas?" The answer is so simple and yet so complicated.

Ideas come from life. They come from everywhere: personal experiences, news clippings, TV talk shows, words to a song, overheard conversations, twists on other stories. The list is endless. Many writers dream complete or partial plots for novels. One thing is certain: The more you work at being a writer, the more easily new plot ideas spring into your mind.

When I began the plot outline for my first novel, the scenes formed in my head with some difficulty because plotting was new to me. I recall telling a friend that I had to sell this book . . . because I would *never* be able to think of another book-length plot. But before the novel was finished, I came up with ideas for four more novels. This seems to be the rule among writers, rather than the exception. Now my files bulge with fragments of story lines for future novels. Some of these will form the basis for a complete novel; in other cases, two or more ideas will combine to create a single, more intricate plot. But should the day arrive when I can't think of an idea for another book, having a file of ideas to consider could help to prevent writer's block.

Something to Hang Your Book On
To start a novel from scratch you must find something to hang your book on. Some writers call it "a germ of an idea." It could evolve out of a character, an incident, an event, a career, a setting, a title, or even a documented or well-known fact. *Anything that triggers an emotional or physical response or action can provide the foundation for a novel.*

When I wrote *The Coventry Courtship*, a Harlequin Regency Romance novel, I became so intrigued with the characters that I didn't want to let them go. I adored my outrageous Udora, who at age thirty had been widowed five times and was currently unattached. It was noted that each of her husbands had died with a smile on his face. When she inherited the Thackery Jewels, they proved to be three young girls—Amethyst, Emerald, and Topaz Thackery. *The Coventry Courtship* told how Udora found love in unexpected places while accepting the responsibilities thrust upon her.

The sequel, a trilogy called *The Thackery Jewels*, is the coming-of-age story of the three girls and their quest to follow their hearts while also trying to follow the dictates of Society. It was a young woman's duty to snare a husband who was not only titled, but also able to provide her with all the material goods that were considered crucial in the glittering world of the Regency era.

Using that as a universal problem, I gave each of the girls a character tag that motivated her behavior. Amethyst was softhearted. She could never pass by a creature or person in need without attempting to help them. She was the perfect target for a woman who abandoned her newborn baby.

Emerald was intelligent, a bluestocking bookworm. It was unlikely that any man would offer for her under those conditions. But the hero, needing a wife to bear him an heir, foolishly made a wager that changed his life most alarmingly. Or so he thought.

Emerald and Amethyst were twins. Topaz, their adopted sister, was born with an adventurous spirit. Her love of ballooning, coupled with her drive to find her real parents, plunged her into one adventure after another until she accomplished her greatest feat—capturing the man of her dreams.

Using the Regency setting, as well as the restrictions which society imposed on people of that day, provided a perfect foundation on which to hang the plot. The conflict, of course, arose from those restrictions as well as the character quirks, flaws and goals that distinguished each character from the others.

Trisha Alexander, who has twenty-six contemporary romances to her name, says her ideas come from everywhere. "It's so ironic," she said. "For years I put off starting to write because I didn't have a clue where I'd get an idea to write about, but once I actually began to write, the ideas came so fast, I knew I wouldn't live long enough to write them all. Other ideas have been triggered by newspaper articles, songs, movies, poems, and other books."

Mother of the Groom was triggered by watching her oldest daughter be fitted for her wedding gown. The idea for another novel, *The Girl Next Door*, came from a reader who asked her if she'd ever thought of writing a story about best friends who fall in love. The plot for *Substitute Bride* unfolded after a friend mentioned how much she loved to read stories of identical twins. All three books are from Silhouette Special Editions, Silhouette Books.

Irma Ruth Walker, author of many romance, mystery, historical and mainstream novels, says: "Most of my ideas come from my own life— or my strong personal interests. I find there's an added depth to those books that arise from personal experience."

Jayne Ann Krentz, who also writes under the name Amanda Quick, is a writer in constant demand. "I always imagine a scene of intense emotional conflict between a man and a woman first," Krentz explains. "This is my starting point. That scene generates everything else, including characterization and the plot elements necessary to allow me to develop that point of conflict."

You can use almost any event to hang a story on: a hurricane, a county fair, a wedding, a business conference, a crime scene, a family reunion, the reading of a will, or flea market day at the fairgrounds. The possibilities are endless. One way to get started is to make a list of all the things that interest you: gardening, sports, history, the cinema, science, psychology, travel, castles, nature, geology, animals, etc.

In a monthly column on fiction I wrote for *The Writers Connection*, I stated that you can take any major Sunday newspaper and find ideas for five novels. A reader challenged me, so the following month I had to prove my point. Here's what I found.

1. Heading: Boy playing with handgun accidentally shoots, kills girl.
It's always wise to change situations to protect everyone. To dramatize this story, I might make the protagonist a girl who killed her mother, but recalled later that her father had convinced her that she was guilty,

knowing that she would not go to prison, but he, as the true murderer, would be sentenced to death.

2. Heading: For sale: 1 Cloister With View. The article is based on the story of an order of nuns who are trying to sell a convent that was once the site of a school for prospective nuns. The possibilities are endless. This story could be a romantic suspense with a "ticking clock" element, or a "quest to find a home for the homeless" romance novel, or a power struggle romance.

3. Heading: Los Gatos Mountains Open Home Tour. This is a generic real estate ad. What sets it apart is that the home is situated in an isolated, upscale community. You meet some really weird people in the real estate business. This story could be a romantic suspense novel . . . where the heroine discovers a letter taped to the bottom of a closet shelf, or it could be a comedy involving conflict between the hero and heroine who try to sabotage each other's sale.

4. Heading: Another You? This article illustrates the complicated realities of human cloning. It would make an interesting futuristic novel in a world where cloning is commonly accepted.

5. Heading: Dogs Found. It's a generic lost and found ad, but the possibilities are obvious. You could plot a children's story about a lost dog, either from the child's viewpoint or that of the dog.

With the last heading, you might also consider the complexities of a science fiction/horror story. If I were to plot this story, I would use details from a previous Sunday newspaper article to flesh it out. Suppose a family has lost its cherished family dog. They go to the pound only to be told that the dog has been euthanized. The family wants to claim the remains. When the attendant opens the freezer, the dog is found, still alive (that part is fact from the newspaper). Eventually they discover there is an implant in the dog's brain. Is it an alien dog-abduction story? A military experiment gone wrong? Was the device planted there by a benign healer? Or does the implant match a metal plate that had been implanted in her husband's head following an auto accident? The husband died a few months later. Is he back? You take it from there.

Four words should be uppermost in your mind: *What would happen if?* These words can trigger ideas for a limitless number of plots because the question, *what if*, must be answered according to the emotional responses of the characters in direct relationship to his or her individual personality. No event has any meaning until there are characters present to react to that event.

Elizabeth Lowell (who uses the pen names Ann Maxwell and A.E. Maxwell when writing with her husband) says that all of her novels are born from that simple question: *What if?* Lowell stresses the importance of careful selection of careers for both the hero and the heroine. "I use professions as character metaphors; it allows me to accomplish at least two things at once. The older the character, the more important a role the character's profession has in my novels, for I believe that the choice of a profession reveals much about a person. You know you have the right profession and background for a character when you can't change the back story, setting or occupation without substantially altering both character and plot development."

Careers can reflect a character's personality as well as create conflict through that character's professional goals. In choosing careers for your primary characters, select wisely. Learn enough about the profession to make the story sound authentic and logical, yet don't lose sight of the fact that the focus of the novel is on the romance.

Have fun with those words: *What if.* What would happen if the heroine forgot to have the papers recorded at the courthouse? What would happen if the protagonist missed the departing tour bus? What would happen if the baby she brought home from the hospital belonged to someone else? What would happen if she overheard a threatening conversation in an adjoining booth? What would happen if she took the wrong plane? What would happen if she were caught by a television camera and someone recognized her from a past she was trying to conceal?

What if is the basis for most brainstorming sessions. As you exercise your creative muscles, they become stronger and more flexible. The process works for one person but is even more dynamic when a group of people brainstorms a single idea. This is another advantage of belonging to a small, compatible workshop group.

Professional writers are frequently collectors. An idea box divided into sections labeled character profiles, incidents, interesting facts, careers, places, newspaper clippings, titles, famous quotes, etc., can be a gold mine for creating plot hangers. Better yet, use a computerized database to organize your information.

Once you have the foundation for an idea, you must start to develop the characters whose lives will be put in jeopardy as the story unfolds. Ask yourself, *What conflicts will arise out of the developing story? What do the characters have to gain or lose during the development? How and why will it change their lives? How can I make this story different, more dramatic than similar stories written around this subject? And how can I shape this story to fit a particular romance line?* These are all vital questions which can and will affect the salability of your romance novel.

Some authors begin to structure their novel by writing down key scenes that have strong emotional impact. Think about the scenes as if you were watching a film. When you can see the scenes in your mind's eye, can feel their impact, then you know the scenes have strong dramatic possibilities. Don't be concerned about the order in which they appear. The scenes can be moved around as the story progresses. The characters may evolve out of the scene or the scene out of the characters. Either one can be a starting point.

Once you have the characters well in hand and you have an idea for the theme and the major conflict, you can begin to write a *synopsis* (a narrative description) or an *outline* (a scene-by-scene breakdown of each chapter). This step helps you determine when you have enough plot to fill the necessary number of pages. Your market research will tell you how many pages you need. If novels published in the line for which you want to write average 75,000 words, then you know you must be able to fill three hundred manuscript pages. In the chapter on plotting, we will delve further into the subject of developing your basic plot into a book-length story.

It never fails to amaze even experienced writers how often another writer will come up with an almost identical plot when there is no chance that the idea could have been stolen. Perhaps the reason is that popular subjects are the inspiration for many novels. When the idea of surrogate motherhood became popular, a number of authors leapt on the subject as a basis for conflict. Other authors have come up with plot ideas by reading Ann Landers's columns, so it is not unusual to find similarities. There is no sure way to protect yourself, but the professional approach is to read recent releases or at least read the reviews in newsletters such as *Affaire de Coeur* and *Romantic Times* to see what has been done and to become familiar with all areas of the genre. Then, when a great idea occurs to you, don't waste too much time in sending off your proposal, or someone may get there first.

Exercises

Note: Exercises are not for everyone. For those writers who find that exercises stimulate understanding of writing techniques, a few suggestions follow.

1. Make a list of "what-would-happen-if" situations to be filed away for later use.

2. Spend a day alone browsing at random through the library. Make a note of the subjects and books that interest you. Explore biographies and autobiographies, geography books, career books, diaries, old history books, and special interest books on topics like stamp collecting, jewelry making, transportation or music. List characters who might fit into a book inspired by your research.

3. Investigate the Internet looking for trends and subject matter. This is a superb research tool, which is extremely quick and easy.

4. Collect people: both their personalities and their experiences. Watch talk shows. Everyone has a story to tell. First-person articles in magazines can trigger plot points for a novel and give marvelous insight into character.

3

Point of View

*T*he viewpoint character is the person in the story who has the most to gain or lose through the outcome of the critical situation. It is also the specific character or characters with whom the writer wants the reader to identify. Romance novelists have a choice of using first-person viewpoint, single third-person viewpoint, multiple third-person viewpoint and omniscient viewpoint.

First-Person Viewpoint
First-person stories are *I* stories; that is, the story is told by the protagonist. Here is an example:

> I knew the moment I opened the ancient gate that everything had changed. Marcus was there. He apparently sensed my presence and turned to look at me. My gaze was drawn to his face. He was different somehow. Worry lines edged his eyes and he moved slowly, as if time had ceased to exist. He knows, I thought. He knows all about me. His voice was harsh when he spoke.
>
> "You lied to me," he said. "Why didn't you tell me I have a daughter?"
>
> My throat tightened and I tried to keep my hands from shaking. "Ariel is my child. She has nothing to do with you."
>
> "There was only one divine birth, Adriana." He wiped his hand across his mustache. "Nothing you say will convince me that another man is her father."

First-person viewpoint is used less frequently than it used to be. Rarely is it used in romance novels. Some of the disadvantages are that first person limits the physical mobility of the protagonist. She cannot see herself through another character's thoughts. Therefore, she can only be described through dialogue or through her views of herself. We can know only *her* thoughts, can witness only the action that *she* sees or hears. Otherwise, action that occurs when the heroine is not present must be told to her by another character. First-person stories are single-viewpoint stories. A character cannot be in two places at one time, so the point of view is limited.

Occasionally, first-person viewpoint is used in Young Adult romance novels, Gothics and mysteries, but many editors and readers dislike the technique. Consequently, a novel written in that style can be difficult to sell.

There are other options for the writer who prefers first person viewpoint. Confession stories are always written in the first person. Writing them is an excellent way of training yourself to write strong characterization. Magazine fiction, such as stories published in *Redbook* and *The New Yorker* and many prize-winning literary short stories are frequently written in first person.

The use of first person singular does add a sense of immediacy to the narrative. This justifies using it as a device when an element of mystery is needed, but for most novels, the advantage rarely outweighs the disadvantages. Once a writer develops an ear for the voice of the novel, finding the right viewpoint is comparatively easy. It comes through reading other fiction and experimenting with different viewpoints to see which works best for that particular story.

Single Third-Person Viewpoint

In the history of the genre, most romance novels evolved from first-person viewpoint to third-person viewpoint. In a romance novel, this is the *she* story. An example:

> Katherine knew the moment she opened the ancient gate that everything had changed. Marcus was there. He apparently sensed her presence and turned to look at her. Her gaze was drawn to his face. He was different somehow. Worry lines edged his eyes and he moved slowly as if time had ceased to exist. He knows, she thought. He knows all about me.

Although single third-person viewpoint also limits the writer to using only the viewpoint character's thoughts, the technique is acceptable. Some of the lines with shorter romances prefer single to multiple viewpoint. The main advantage to a single viewpoint is that the writer is allowed to keep secrets from the reader. If we are unable to get into the hero's head, the heroine must anguish over his unexplained actions and feelings. We are only aware of those feelings that he reveals through action or dialogue in her presence. She can only observe and guess at his feelings and motivations.

The following example shows *incorrect* usage of single third-person viewpoint with the heroine as the viewpoint character:

Wrong

Jeremy felt the need to put some distance between them. He wanted to be alone to think over Carolyn's offer.

Better

Carolyn watched Jeremy edge toward the door. It was obvious that he wanted to put some distance between them. He probably needed to be alone to think over her offer.

Multiple Third-Person Viewpoint

The use of both the heroine's viewpoint and the hero's adds significant depth to a novel, and this is a technique that a writer should develop early on. It is the style most commonly used and seems to be most accepted by readers. For romance novels it is usually best to limit the multiple viewpoint to that of the heroine and hero. Keep in mind that the romance is frequently the heroine's story with most of the internalization seen in her viewpoint. There are several new series, however, where the main viewpoint character is the hero. Study the current market to see where your book fits in.

Notice in the following example of two viewpoints that it is very clear to the reader which thoughts belong to Jeremy and which to Carolyn.

Jeremy studied her face. She was putting him on the spot again. Damn her! He loved her but he couldn't let her get away with this. He needed time. Time and space.

Carolyn watched him back slowly toward the door. "This is it, then? You're leaving?" He didn't answer and she knew by the way his face was set in granite that he wanted to put some distance between them.

Purists insist that only one viewpoint should be used per scene, unlike the above example. Too many head hops on a page can be distracting and can result in rejection from an editor who dislikes this style.

Multiple viewpoint has many advantages. By knowing what the hero is thinking, we can delve more deeply into his character and emotional conflicts. We can see the heroine through the hero's eyes and this measurably increases the sexual tension. Although the reader becomes aware of the hero's feelings, the heroine may still remain unaware of his thoughts until he reveals them to her in action or dialogue. By getting into the hero's head we are able to more fully motivate his actions, thereby making them more believable and acceptable.

Here is an example from *Family Ties* (Harlequin Intrigue #444) by Joanna Wayne. This is a secret-baby story with an element of intrigue. The hero, a rich politician from Texas, has come to claim the child he just learned was his:

> He didn't have a leg to stand on when it came to taking Petey away from Ashley. Not unless he could prove she was an unfit mother. After seeing her with Petey today, he knew that was out of the question. She was a perfect mother, and he was an out-of-state politician who hadn't known the boy existed until a day ago. That's why he had to get her to Texas.
>
> He didn't trust her. If she had her way he'd be heading back to the ranch right now believing Petey wasn't his. He would have known, though, even if Petey hadn't been branded liberally with Randolph features.

Study the preceding paragraphs to understand the wealth of information fed so discreetly to the reader. It could have been done in direct dialogue or straight narration, but by giving the reader an opportunity to get inside the hero's head, the author reveals more about the character. She makes the hero seem sympathetic by having him recognize that Ashley is a good mother. We also discover that he feels deprived, having not known his son until now. It is also good to note the use of the word branded; it ties in so appropriately with the Texas setting.

Omniscient Viewpoint

The omniscient viewpoint is a necessity for certain types of novels where the story must be viewed from several different angles. It applies mainly to the longer length of single title, mainstream and literary novels where the focus goes beyond the hero and the heroine. Novels where an event such as a flood or a funeral or a convention is really the main focus may require this viewpoint. The plot evolves out of each character's reaction to the event and how that event affects their lives before, during and after the primary action takes place.

If the story is to be told through the eyes of more than two characters, one technique is to use one viewpoint character per chapter. Chapter one might be David's story; chapter two, Helen's story; chapter three, Arnold's story, and so on. This technique gives the writer a chance to fully develop the characters, so the reader knows them before moving on to the next chapter and character.

One rule applies to both omniscient and multiple third-person viewpoint: The writer must clearly identify who the viewpoint character is at that moment. When there are more than two people in the room or when there is dialogue that continues for several paragraphs, you cannot rely on unattributed thoughts or delay too long in identifying the speaker. In this type of situation the use of body language or character tags, (see chapter five), can be beneficial in keeping the reader aware of who is speaking.

Wrong

"We could spend the afternoon at the lake, then go to the casino after dinner," Tom said.

"Let's have dinner at the casino," Steve suggested. "It will save time."

"No. I need to go home and change clothes before I go to the casino," Helen said.

Better

Tom opened the newspaper to the entertainment section. "We could spend the afternoon at the lake, then go to the casino after dinner."

Steve consulted his watch. "Let's have dinner at the casino. It will save time. Whada ya say, Helen?"

"Don't be silly. I need to go home and change clothes before I can go to the casino."

The choice of a viewpoint character, or characters, can strengthen or weaken the novel and its salability. First, read the publisher's guidelines and research the line to which you plan to submit in order to learn which viewpoint they most commonly use. Then try writing your story in that viewpoint. It should work. If it doesn't, perhaps you are slanting the story toward the wrong market. If you find you are committed to a viewpoint that differs from the editorial guidelines, you might try submitting a synopsis and sample chapters. Editorial guidelines are not carved in granite; if a book is truly exceptional, an editor might take a chance on it. For the unpublished author, however it is best to follow the rules.

Exercise

Read romance novels from the publisher's line which most appeals to you. Study the narration and internal dialogue to discover in which viewpoint the book is written. For practice, take a page where more than one character is present and write the page in a different viewpoint.

4

The Characters

*N*o matter which romance line you choose to write for, there is one unbreakable rule: The focus of the story must be the developing relationship between the heroine and the hero. Even when using both viewpoints, it's usually the heroine who is the main viewpoint character (though these days, the hero frequently plays the major role). Since most of the story will be seen through the viewpoint character's eyes, you must carefully select players who will both complement and contrast with each other. That contrast must be strong enough to act as a catalyst for conflict, yet the characters must be similar enough in their personalities to be irrevocably drawn to each other despite their differences.

Many authors create character charts or list the various traits of the main characters in order to see the intricacies of their relationship as expressed through opposing or complementary personality quirks. There is another advantage to keeping a character chart. When you first begin writing, it is very easy to remember names and descriptions. However, as you progress from chapter to chapter and book to book, you will soon discover how easy it is to forget names, as well as color of hair or eyes. By charting or listing the physical as well as psychological makeup of your characters, you will save time and effort. You will also avoid changing your character's vital statistics midway through the book. A pair of sample character charts is located at the end of this chapter.

The Heroine: A Profile According to Category

Before you begin to draw the profiles of the characters for your story, you must thoroughly study the publisher's guidelines and read romances that have been *recently* released by that house. Readers complain if too many books come out with similar characters or the same setting. Publishers listen to reader comments and are sure to reject a book if they think readers will resist it.

Most romance books can be placed into one of two broad categories: the traditional romance or the sophisticated romace. The kind of heroine you find in a Harlequin Romance has a different personality profile from the heroine in a Zebra Romance or a Harlequin Temptation Romance. You will find not only an age difference but opposing views on life. This fact supports the argument for careful market research before you begin to write. The time and frustration you save will be well worth it.

In traditional or sweet romances, where more importance is placed on *sensuality* than *sexuality*, the heroine is younger—usually in her late twenties or thirties—and is comparatively inexperienced sexually. In Harlequin's Virginal Heroine line, for example, the heroine is most likely to be in her mid- to late twenties. The values she holds are traditional. She must be bright and likable with a sense of her own worth. She must have character depth that surfaces in times of crisis and have the capability of growing in character. A career is optional. She may be self-employed, have a successful career outside the home or be a full-time mother.

Of all the romance lines, the traditional romances lend themselves to the Cinderella-type story or fantasy more easily than the more sophisticated, self-made success stories of the longer, more sensual novels. According to a panel of Silhouette editors, some themes that continue to be popular in traditional romances are the arranged marriage, cowboys, and secret babies.

The heroine in the more sophisticated romance lines can be older, usually in her thirties and occasionally even forties. The age difference can reflect her sense of worldliness. She may have already found her niche in the working scene, or she is well on her way to success. This does not mean that she must have a high-powered or glamorous career. She could be a teacher or a salesperson as easily as a nuclear scientist, but she should feel good about herself and have an optimistic outlook on life. Although she may want to have a marriage and a family, this is only one side of her more complex personality. She should have other interests and goals. Romance heroines are never promiscuous.

One mistake beginning authors make regarding the importance of career in romance novels is making the heroine a corporate genius at age nineteen, with little or no previous work experience. It is true that romance novels lean toward fantasy, but it must be fantasy based on believability. If the characters do not ring true, the reader will neither believe the characters nor identify with them.

The older, very mature woman is occasionally featured as a heroine, but the book must be exceptional for it to be accepted. A few publishers have experimented with senior citizen romances, but the lines have not survived. Such characters work well for secondary roles.

The Hero: A Profile According to Category

The romantic hero is also created according to the demands of the individual romance lines. The traditional romances, such as Harlequin Romance, sell widely to foreign women who like their heroes more domineering and their heroines less outspoken. For this reason the hero in the traditional romance is usually a little older than the heroine. It is wise to avoid the very extreme age differences between hero and heroine that were once so popular.

Our traditional hero is sometimes in a position of great wealth, possessing the ability to wield the power that goes with it. However, the hero could also be a single parent who must cope with all the problems and responsibilities of that lifestyle. He will have flaws, but we still admire him for his strength and basic goodness. Above all, the reader must fall in love with him.

In the more sensual romance novels, such as Silhouette Desire, the hero is allowed a wider range of development, but no matter how gritty the character, he must have a basic integrity. His age should be compatible with the age of the heroine.

Although sensitivity is a welcome character trait for the romance hero, the writer must *never* allow the hero to be a wimp. Nor should any man with whom the heroine was romantically involved be too wimpish or too boorish. As one editor told me, "It doesn't say much for the heroine's taste or judgment if she was engaged to a man who is a total reject. You have to give him a character flaw that turns her off yet is not so obvious that friends would laugh at her for dating him."

For these more sensual lines the hero can be anything from a garage mechanic to a cop to a multimillionaire industrialist. His personality can range from boyish to professorial depending on his career and his background. But he must have one outstanding characteristic: To the heroine, the hero must exude masculinity. That doesn't mean he has to be handsome, debonair and have the body of an athlete. When the heroine sees him, something about him simply triggers a primal instinct in her that "sends the blood rushing through her veins."

Do not rely only upon physical attraction to hold your characters together. Although sexuality works as a fine catalyst, the chemistry of love demands a deeper, multidimensional relationship to make the romance thrive. It may be a shared interest; a common goal or an opposing goal; a need, such as someone to help combat loneliness; or it may simply be that the characters have fun together. Whatever it is, the characters must be drawn to each other by some compelling emotion, be it love or hate, then recognize their physical need for each other—a need that culminates in a desire for a permanent commitment.

You cannot write an engrossing romance novel until you create a heroine with whom the reader wants to identify and a hero with whom the reader can fall in love. Neither can be omitted.

They are not true-to-life characters, though on the surface they might appear to be. They are idealized. The heroine is someone women would like to emulate: nicer, prettier, thinner, more intelligent, though not necessarily all of those things. She will have a flaw, but it will be a minor one. We know at the start of the novel that our heroine will ultimately find happiness beyond compare. Unlike the "woman next door," the heroine cannot be attracted to more than one man at one time.

Drugs, child abuse and other such issues must be used with caution and only for certain lines. Rape is rarely used as a device in relationship to the heroine. Issues run in cycles. Study current guidelines to see what editors will accept. You can push the envelope to a certain extent, but there are limits. More and more, editors are looking for innovative authors who dare to push guidelines to the extreme and still meet the publisher's requirements.

The hero is the ideal lover and husband and father. He does not have to be rich, though we know he could be if he set his mind to it. He doesn't have to be the most handsome man our heroine has ever seen, but he should have at least one physical quality that is outstanding—preferably one that is visible when he is fully clothed.

Above all, he must be the man with whom every woman would like to fall in love. A romance editor once said that three things make a great romance novel: (1) a hero to die for, (2) a hero to die for, (3) a hero to die for.

Both hero and heroine must have personal goals. Of course, if the premise of your story is that one of the characters has no purpose in life, that character must grow and mature until he or she finds that elusive ideal for which he or she has been searching.

Building warm, believable, compelling characters is a challenge and a delight. They are the strength of your novel. Creating characters is like weaving a tapestry. If the strands are weak, the fabric will fall apart. If they are colorless, the fabric will be unappealing. If they are lifeless and one-dimensional, the fabric will have no substance.

Secondary Characters

Once the heroine becomes involved with the hero, there can be no other man for her. This does not mean she doesn't have other friends. A man and woman do not exist in a void before or after they discover each other. To make their relationship percolate, it is always helpful to have secondary characters who counterbalance the sexual tension and act as a sounding board for the main characters' insights and feelings. Although we keep the hero and heroine together as much as possible, there are advantages to giving them someone in whom they can confide. It gives us an opportunity to insert motivation cues and explain plot points through dialogue instead of narration or introspection.

When romance novels first became popular, the roommate or maiden aunt dutifully filled this position, but those characters have become cliché. Those were also the days when we killed off the parents, usually in an auto accident or a plane crash, so the heroine would be comparatively helpless and alone in the world.

Changing attitudes toward the role of women in society have made it acceptable for a woman to choose to be independent. It is no longer necessary to make our heroine an orphan to justify her living away from home. Now the secondary character may be a best friend, a co-worker or even a family member.

At one time, putting children into a story was the kiss of death. Now, according to a panel of Harlequin editors, the classic story lines of secret babies, single parents, amnesia and arranged marriages are among the most popular, particularly in the traditional romances. Although a child can be the catalyst that draws the heroine and hero together, the writer must be careful not to let the child take over the entire story.

Although additional characters can serve a specific purpose, it is wise to avoid cluttering the stage. The purpose of a secondary character is to fill a need that cannot easily be taken over by an existing character. If an existing character can double up to fill the role, consider this solution. To overpopulate a novel with superfluous characters is not only poor writing, but it also confuses the reader, who will need a scorecard to keep the players separate.

Avoiding Cliché Characters

When you consider the number of romance novels that have been published, it must seem impossible to create a character who is not already a cliché. If you think merely in terms of labels, that statement could be true. By labels, I mean nurse, artist, teacher, reporter, scientist, actress, homemaker, secretary and every other profession that pigeonholes a character into a traditional woman's role or a particular mindset.

At one time, career nursing was one of the few professions open to women. The same limitations were placed on heroines in books, and, as a result, some publishing houses devoted nearly their entire line to books featuring a nurse as the protagonist. Thomas Bouregy, Inc., a small publisher of hardcover books primarily for school libraries, is one example. Many romance writers were published in a Bouregy hardcover before moving to paperback houses like Dell or Harlequin. Bouregy (Avalon Books) still offers romance novels, but the line has expanded to include other careers while still preserving the message of squeaky clean morals.

Along about 1995, the heroes of some romance lines took on grittier personalities. Today almost anything goes, but there are pitfalls for those who don't study the specific requirements. Some professions do not work well for today's romance markets. Readers, for some unexplained reason, reject novels dealing with careers in the ballet, theater, cinema, the arts and sports. As a result, editors almost always reject these backgrounds.

As romance novels move closer to mainstream, the characters are less likely to be larger than life. Silhouette Special Editions often features heroines and heroes who are small-town-boy or girl-next-door types with problems even the least sophisticated reader can relate to. Still, there must be some quality that sets those characters apart and draws the characters, not only to each other, but to the reader.

In Alicia Scott's novel, *Maggie's Man* (Silhouette Intimate Moments #776), the hero, Cain, dressed as a prison guard, kidnaps the heroine and then steals a truck.

Suzanne Brockman chose an ex-Navy SEAL who was badly crippled to be the hero of *Frisco's Kid* (Silhouette Intimate Moments #759).

Anne Stuart created Simon of Navarre, "a powerful and mysterious lord practiced in the black arts" for *Lord of Danger*, a Zebra historical. Romance heroes must be compelling, romance heroines must be strong, but, most of all, the characters must be motivated and sympathetic so the reader can identify with them.

So how does a writer select his characters? There are several solutions. Be creative. If you must write about a nurse, let her be unusual. How about a nurse who travels across country with a high school debate team? Or take the ordinary perception of a career and turn it around. For example, why not let the hero be the nurse and let the heroine be the patient, or the doctor? Another way to give your character depth is to create a problem that's almost too difficult to solve. To select a character without a problem is to write a story without drama.

If your character is inappropriate but you are still committed to him, a third solution might be to hold the manuscript until the pendulum swings back and the cliché becomes the unusual again. But the best solution of all is to create warm, likable protagonists who are faced with realistic and sustained conflicts, which they resolve satisfactorily at the conclusion of the book.

Writing salable characters is a skill that can be learned. It takes practice and a sensitivity toward people and what makes them tick. Once you've mastered the basic requirements for heroines, heroes and secondary characters, you can delve into the various techniques of bringing those characters to life.

Exercises

Study recently published romance novels. Underline in one color highlighter pen everything you can learn about the heroine: age, physical description, background, motivation. Choose other colored pens for the hero and one or two secondary characters and do the same thing.

Copy the character charts that follow and fill out one for each important character and for his or her family background. Much of the information will not be used in the context of the story but it will help you to understand your characters.

Family Background Chart

character's name

ethnic origin

physical appearance

attitude toward other characters

professions/education

economic status/lifestyle

religious status/ethics code

hobbies/avocations

health status if living; if not, tell details of death

close relatives: their age and relationship to character

Main Character

character's name _____

height _____ age _____ eyes _____ hair _____ shape _____

self-image _____ health _____

education _____ goals (personal) _____

profession _____ goals (career) _____

code of ethics _____

religious attitudes _____

financial situation _____

responsibilities/commitments _____

marital status and attitude _____

relationship to others _____

hobbies/other interests _____

fears/apprehensions _____

yearnings _____

sense of humor _____

surroundings/environment _____

habits and quirks _____

favorite foods/favorite color _____

positive traits/strengths _____

negative traits/weaknesses _____

5

How to Make Your Characters Come to Life

The secret to writing a salable romance novel lies in creating strong, believable, likable and sympathetic characters. Think about it. The romance novels you reread and refuse to part with are the books with the most memorable characters. It's the people who make up 70 percent of the story. The other 30 percent is plot. This rule holds true for most fiction. Even if the novel revolves around a mystery or a problem, there must be characters who ultimately will be affected by the outcome of the critical situation and the conflict.

One of the most common reasons for rejection is the author's failure to bring the characters to life.

Irma Ruth Walker said, "I create my characters—I'd rather call them 'people'—from the inside out. Only when they come alive to me, when I know how they think and where they are coming from, do I worry about their physical appearance. To me, they all exist somewhere in this world—or in another."

I read once that no one can know a person better than the person himself, because it's what he does in private, when no one is watching, that determines his true character. Think about that when you are defining your characters.

Beyond External Qualities

To build a character, you must go far beyond the visual, external qualities an individual possesses. Mixing together all the material attributes in a human system—hair color and eye color and body shape—does not make a person. If we limit the descriptions of our characters to the visual, we fail to bring our characters to life.

When an editor tells you your people are too slight or too shallow or lack depth, she means you have failed to delve deeply into their *psychological* makeup to give them *cause* for their behavior.

We cannot create believable, sympathetic characters without giving the reader a clue as to their backgrounds. Only in science fiction does a character appear on earth out of thin air. We all are multifaceted personalities—products of genetic evolution, past and present environments, and the fates that shape our individuality.

Character is created through a *layering process* that develops over a period of years, rather than through a single set of circumstances. To create believable characters, we must establish a past history for them. These layers consist of a multitude of influences such as race, nationality, economic status, religious background, family life, health, and many more.

Take, for example, two women. Each was reared as an only child in a wealthy home. Both grew up in California during the late 1960s. Both are attractive and intelligent. Now consider how their lives would evolve if one of the women, Katy, was reared by nurturing parents who wanted nothing but the best for her, whereas the other woman, Stella, was brought up by parents who were cold and uncaring. To take it even farther, Katy's mother may have been a nursery school teacher who adored children, but Stella's mother was an actress who didn't want the world to know she was old enough to have a grown daughter.

Remember that you can make your people do anything as long as you properly motivate them. By digging through the layers of their personalities, you can discover how they would act or react to a situation. These details compose the fundamental traits of a character's identity and reveal his or her motivation.

Katy may rebel against her upbringing and become a permissive parent because she felt she was smothered by family affection, or she might be true to her upbringing and become the perfect parent.

Stella also has the choice of turning away from her family and making a decent life for herself because she learned from their mistakes. Or, she could follow her parents' example and end up as a cold person. The choice depends on the roles they play within the context of the plot. These twists and turns in the players' development keep a story from being predictable. This also explains how twenty different people can take the same basic characters and write a thousand different plots.

Character development charts such as the ones on pages 33-34 will help you brainstorm ideas to further develop the characters in your romance novel or short story. Be careful to choose only relevant information so your reader is not besieged with details that slow the momentum of the story.

Debbie Macomber, a multipublished author, said "It's impossible to create a vibrant, excited character unless you know what motivates that person. To do that, I've constructed a profile in reverse. Instead of collecting background information on a character, I decide how that particular character will react in any given situation, keeping the plot in mind.

"An example of this would be the spider on the kitchen floor. My heroine sees the spider. How will she react? She can ignore the silly thing and pray it will be gone when she returns. She can squish it with her shoe and hurriedly kick it out of sight. Or she could squish it, get it into the sink, turn on the faucet and garbage disposal, and grind it up for five minutes until she is absolutely certain it's dead. Or she can phone the hero, tell him she's in grave danger and insist he come and rescue her.

"Once I have an idea how my character will react to a variety of everyday incidents, I walk him or her through the plot scene by scene and decide on the appropriate reaction."

Another device many writers use to better see their cast of players is to cut pictures out of catalogs or magazines of people who resemble those players. If you hang the pictures in front of your typewriter or computer so you can see them while you work, you will imprint those characters in your mind, and they will be less difficult to describe.

So, how does one create characters who will remain in the reader's thoughts long after the book is finished? There are many ways to show strong characterization. Here are seven suggestions.

1. Show Characterization Through Direct Narrative Description

Be careful of this one. It is easy to get carried away with telling what is happening, rather than showing. The problem is that you lose immediacy and remove the reader a step away from the action. If used with discretion, narration can be an asset to characterization, as in the following excerpt from *The Honeymoon Deal* by Kate Hoffman (Harlequin Temptation Romance #627).

The white-haired matron was dressed as she always was—in cabbage roses. From the fabric of her dress to the decorations on her shoes, even springing from the ever-present hat perched on her head, cabbage roses of all shapes, sizes and colors seemed to envelop her. If that didn't constitute floral overload, Eunice's office was bedecked with the same fussy flowers, always leaving Lianne craving an elegant stripe or a simple check—or a bottle of aphid killer.

Note that the unusually long sentences in themselves may be considered a device. Shorter, tighter description would not have achieved the same effect. If a writer is describing a lean, athletic type, the tone and length of each sentence would instead be lean and strong.

In *Bride Of The Sheikh* (Silhouette Intimate Moments #771), author Alexandra Sellers describes how the heroine, Alinor, is kidnapped during her wedding by Kavian, who claims she is still married to him. In this scene he has picked her up and faces the assembled guests.

Everything stopped while that moment was recorded in time: the image of the white-robed prince, his skin tanned by the desert sun, his deep green eyes hard, his teeth bared in a smile of triumph and daring; in his arms a woman of pale, delicate beauty, a circlet of flowers on her brow, her ash-coloured hair tangled but flowing over the dark strong fingers that held her, her white silk skirt and the flowers she held falling in a mingled swathe to the floor, her eyes icy with fury. Behind them the rose window glowed with complementary colours of white, rose and blue. To the assembled, touched by wonder, they seemed a work of art.

Light, color, mood, setting—all these elements are tools the author uses to set this very visual scene through the use of narration.

2. Show Characterization Through Dialogue

Dialogue is perhaps the most powerful tool for defining character to be found in the author's box of illusions. Rejections are often based on the author's inability to write believable and appropriate dialogue. For this reason, an entire chapter will be devoted to writing dialogue.

3. Show Characterization Through Introspection

Used judiciously, *introspection* (the character's unspoken thoughts) can enhance characterization by letting us see into the viewpoint person's mind. Example:

> Diane knew that Jason and Holly had never met but she detected a flicker of recognition in their eyes when she introduced them. She knew instantly that they were kindred souls. Takers.
>
> They were on their way up; clever, bright, and shallow as a saucer half filled with cream. And like the predators they were, they didn't give a damn about who the cream belonged to. It was theirs for the taking.
>
> There was no doubt in Diane's mind that this meeting would mark "finished" between her and Jason. She envied them their self-assurance, yet another part of her was glad that she had been brought up to respect the feelings of others. There was no way she could live with herself if she tried to play the game by their rules.

Through introspection we can understand how characters relate to others and we can begin to understand why the person feels as she does about those characters. In short, motivation. Knowing the private workings of a person's mind is like finding a key to the soul.

Flashes of introspection can also provide descriptions of others, thereby avoiding the cliché scene where the heroine sees herself in a mirror or shop window and thinks: *God, I'm beautiful, with my red hair streaming down my back, and my eyes shining clear and blue as a summer sky. My figure is great enough to . . .* Well, you get the picture.

One of my favorite reasons for using introspection is to have the ability to assess the heroine through the hero's eyes. It can strengthen the heroine by letting us know how much he cares for her, but it can also make a hero sympathetic, a hero who otherwise has negative traits that the author has yet to explain away or justify.

Editors do warn us not to "rehash scenes" that have been adequately covered through dialogue or action. Those redundant scenes usually take place while the heroine is in the shower or just falling asleep. They go something like this:

> Diane rolled over on her back and studied the patch of light on the ceiling as she thought about what Paul had said. Did he

really love her? Would it be right for her to give up everything she had worked for just to be with him? She turned on her side, punching the pillow into a ball. He said there was no reason to put it in writing but she wondered.

Instead, if you feel you must establish her uncertainty, you can use direct dialogue with Paul instead of rehashed introspection.

"I've thought about it, Paul, so much that it kept me awake most of the night. . . ."

Or simply allude to her problem with a line or two of transition:

The conversation with Paul and her uncertainty over what to do kept Diane awake most of the night. When the alarm clock finally rang . . .

Introspection must serve a purpose beyond the passing of time. She may, for example, recall a word or phrase spoken earlier. That bit of dialogue may prove to be a clue that solves the crime. Even so, keep the introspection short and intersperse action within it.

4. Show Characterization Through Actions and Reactions

The course of action we take is a direct result of how our personalities have been programmed. In delineating our characters we must always make certain that they stay within character. Everything they do and everything they think must be compatible with the way they have lived their lives. Their attitudes may adjust as they grow and mature but their basic philosophy of life will probably remain the same.

By showing a character in action, we let the reader see another side of that character's personality. The same holds true for reaction, which is similar to action but is usually more sudden, following a specific stimulus.

In the book *Family Ties* by Joanna Wayne (Harlequin Intrigue #444), Ashley and her son, Petey, have been on the run since her brother was killed while involved in a holdup. The robber assumes she has a large share of the money. Ashley's husband, Dillon, was shot and wounded just moments after their wedding ceremony. Shortly after that, he walked out on the marriage, unaware that she was pregnant with his child.

Now, two years later, the killer is out to find the money—even if it means Ashley must pay with her life.

> The storm had knocked out the phone, too. Thunder clapped again, and the whole apartment seemed to shake. She sucked in a calming breath. It was probably the storm that was spooking her. Still, Petey was in the next room. She had to protect him at any cost.
> She stood quietly and tried to think. The rain was all she could hear now, beating against the windows. No. There was something else, quieter. Like hushed breathing, low but distinct. She held her breath as the sudden smell of liquor and sweat accosted her senses.

The opening chapters help the reader understand the dichotomy of Ashley's back-street roots as opposed to Dillon's background of wealth and position. Here is an action scene that shows Ashley's love for her son and her courage in protecting him. With her son asleep in the back room, Ashley is being kidnapped.

> He pushed again, this time sending her careening against the edge of the kitchen table. "Out the back way. Real quiet. So I don't have to shoot a brave husband."
> "No, Please. Just leave and come back in the morning. I'll meet you here and we can look for the money together. I promise." She was grasping for any delay she could find.

Remember that you are in control. If it is essential to the story that your character suddenly behave outrageously, you can justify it. Give the character the proper motivation to make his or her actions believable. In this novel, the character's love for her son serves as the catalyst, but the chemistry between Ashley and Dillon is equally compelling.

5. Show Characterization Through Names

The names we bestow upon our characters create pictures in the minds of our readers. They may know someone who has a similar name or they may associate the name with something or someone about whom they have heard. We can control these images up to a point.

It is wise to choose carefully before you become too involved in the book. I'm not good at changing names once my characters begin to breathe. If I'm forced to change a name, the character never seems quite real to me after that.

The names you select can establish your characters in a period of history, a geographic location, and, within reason, a profession. When was the last time you heard of a newborn child named Homer or Clyde or Maude? Those names were very common in the early 1900s, and it is unlikely that they will return to popularity in the near future.

Conversely, the rule of returning cycles is readily apparent when you think about the names people give to their children today. Jason, Sarah, Joshua and Amanda were very popular names at one time. They've come back. In 1986, Michael and Jessica were the most common names given to babies in California. If you wanted to set your novel in the 1940s, you would find that Linda and Paul were popular names at that time. The reference section at the end of this book lists books that tell what names were popular and when. A name-the-baby book that gives the origin and meanings of names can be helpful too. Information is also available from state and federal birth statistics.

If your book is set in the South, you might consider using a double name such as Lucy Mae or Billy Bob. The names Jean Paul and Andre immediately signal French to the reader. These are handy tags that contribute to a character without the writer having to overwrite the book.

Certain surnames are more common in areas settled by large groups of immigrants. Norwegian and Swedish names are very widespread in Wisconsin where large numbers of Scandinavians made their homes. A glance through U.S. and foreign telephone directories at the public library will tell you in an instant what names are currently popular in most large cities.

Some people say names also reflect careers or lifestyles. Think of Dixie, Stella, Wanda and Mabel, and you think: waitress. Think of Roy, Elmo or Jake, and you think: manual labor. Think Michelle, Daphne, Winthrop or Trent, and you think: country club. Of course this is both oversimplification and stereotyping, but it is important to see characters in relationship to their names. While a name can't take the place of characterization, it's an important part of developing believable characters.

I recently discovered how awkward it is to use a given name that ends in s (James) or ce (Janice). In the singular there is no problem, but when you need the plural or possessive form, the name does not read well. I used the name Constance in *The Tart Shoppe* (Harlequin

Regency) and began to regret it before I reached the third chapter. Some names are considered strong names and some are considered weak. Not all people agree on which are which, so you must train your ear to select names that clearly define the role you want your characters to play.

Several Rules Apply in Naming Characters
Don't use two or more given names beginning with the same letter. It is too difficult for the reader to keep the characters separate. (Don't remind me. I know. I was guilty of using Debra, David and Doug in *Midsummer Madness*. Even *I* got confused before the book was finished.)

Don't use peculiar or phony-sounding names unless you're writing science fiction—the reader can suspect you're making fun of her (according to a popular editor).

Don't use long complicated names for the main characters because it becomes tiresome to see them frequently repeated. Save long or foreign-sounding names for functional characters.

Don't, unless it's necessary to the plot, use unisex names spelled the same for both sexes—names such as Chris, Mickey, Nicky, Andy, Tony, Bobby, Terry, Jan, Lee, etc. It is confusing when you read it in the blurb on the back of the book, and it becomes confusing within the context of the story. Above all, avoid the plot ploy where the heroine goes to apply for a job and the male boss is furious because he thought she was a man when he read her unisex name. It has been used in romance novels more times than you can count.

6. Show Characterization Through Similes and Metaphors
A simile is a comparison of two unlike objects using the introductory *like* or *as*: *His face was as wrinkled as a prune that had lain too long in the sun.* Another example: *His face was like a prune.*

A metaphor is a comparison of one object to another by transference of meaning: *His face was a prune that had lain too long in the sun.* Another example: *She was fire, he was ice. When they came together— meltdown.* Well, you get the idea.

Be careful not to use figures of speech that are anachronistic. In a historical novel, you would not write "her hair crackled with static electricity" if electricity had not been discovered. You should not use arctic comparisons if your novel takes place in the tropics.

Similes and metaphors add texture to a novel providing they are not clichés and providing they are appropriate to the story and not too abundant. It's like adding spices to the stew. A little adds zest, a little more is too much. Some editors like similes and metaphors in a romance novel, but other editors consider them purple prose. "He sought the honey that only she could offer as he plunged through the gates of paradise" is an example of a metaphor that might be considered excessive by some editors. Study the books in the line for which you want to write to see what's being done.

From *For the Love Of Pete* by Rosalyn Alsobrook (St. Martin's Paperbacks contemporary romance) here are two examples of a simile: *Pete's jaw dropped like a metal bat on homeplate after a bunt.* And: *His mother had been acting a lot like Tweetie bird in a room filled with Sylvesters.*

And a metaphor: *(She) . . . stared so many angry daggers through her water glass, Pete was surprised it didn't pop a half-dozen leaks.*

7. Show Characterization Through Labels or Tags

A label or tag is a device used to set one character apart from all others in the novel. The device can be an action or a possession or a catchphrase used only by that character. Again, we must carefully avoid clichés, such as the man running his fingers through his hair to show frustration and the woman going shopping for clothing when she is unhappy.

If you find creating a tag difficult, use television as a tool. Most series utilize tags for characters who appear frequently. What would *The Nanny* be without her nasal twang and tight micro-mini skirts? What would Kramer be without his fast slide when he enters Seinfeld's apartment? What would Tim, the tool man from *Home Improvement*, be without his tool belt and his ineptness? And what would Jim Carrey be without his rubber face?

In my novel *The Thackery Jewels*, a Regency trilogy from Harlequin, Emerald was studious. She was rarely seen without a book tucked in the pocket of her skirt. Amethyst was the nurturer who was psychologically unable to resist saving an injured creature, animal or human. Topaz was the adventurous one who would try anything once.

Dialogue tags associated with a single character can make the character visual if the tag is carefully chosen and not used too frequently. It could be a favorite expletive, a word that's mispronounced or misused, a tendency to drop the *g* on words ending in *ing*, or an often repeated phrase like "You catch my drift?" or "So?"

How do you make your characters sympathetic? In romance novels, because the hero and heroine are idealized characters, this element can be of particular importance. There are some simple solutions.

A "Pollyanna" type of character, who sees nothing but the good in everyone, is boring, unlikable and unbelievable. It would be impossible to involve her in any reasonable conflict. So how do we make our heroine exciting, sympathetic and realistic? The answer is to give her character flaws or a universal problem to which most people can relate.

A one-dimensional person has tunnel vision and straight-line emotions. Such a character in a short story or a novel is flat, cardboardlike, and lifeless. Study the character chart (see page 34) to see how we attempt to bring out the various facets of a character's personality.

The bottom of the chart is divided into positive and negative traits. This, when properly filled out, will help you to further understand your characters and make them more sympathetic. Remember that the balance of qualities should fall on the positive side for the hero and heroine. The less heroic the role, the more the balance can shift to the negative. Even the most villainous people should have at least one good point to make them believable.

When you search for negative traits for your hero and heroine, be careful to avoid those that are too negative, too unacceptable for the heroic role. Remember also that any positive trait, when carried to the extreme, can become a negative one. Example: mother love/ smother love.

A Few Character Traits

Positive: likes people; is charitable; honest; attractive; dependable; good sense of humor; sensitive; generous.

Negative: Tendency to be late; lack of drive (hero, in particular, must have a good reason); too much drive (must learn to slow down or redirect that drive); antisocial (must show strong justification and grow in character); too inflexible (must learn to compromise); limited sense of humor (must learn to laugh); too curious.

Here are some questions you might ask about your characters:

1. What things are important to this character, emotionally as well as physically: career, creature comforts, companionship, etc.?

2. Who or what has had the greatest influence on this character's life? Consider both negative and positive influences.
3. What does this character have to gain from the outcome of the critical situation and conflict? Remember that the protagonist, or viewpoint character, must have the most at stake.
4. What worries or depresses this character?
5. In whom does he or she confide? Who does he trust/distrust?
6. How does this character handle or react to disappointment, defeat, happiness, being alone (does he cherish solitude or does he constantly need to be surrounded by people)?
7. In a few words, tell your character's outlook on life. Does he feel that if you live by the book, life will be good to you? Or does he believe you only live once and you'll miss something if you don't learn to break a few rules?

Once you've created the characters, they are in your hands to manipulate as you please. But if you want the reader to accept them, you must know your characters well enough to predict how they will act or react in any given situation. Once you've achieved this, you'll discover what writers mean when they say their characters took over the book.

A Checklist for Creating Compelling Characters

1. Establish reader identification with your characters as close to the opening as possible.
2. Avoid the confusion of having too many characters. Instead, combine the roles and functions of two characters and let one do the work of two.
3. For maximum conflict and drama, look for characters who sharply contrast each other.
4. Give your reader someone to love, someone to hate.
5. Think visually. Give your characters visible traits or tags.
6. Make your characters perform instead of just letting them sit there. Don't *tell* about your characters. *Show*, through the use of action scenes, who your characters are.
7. Use dialogue wisely and in balance with narration and body language.
8. Avoid overuse of metaphors and similes. Be original in your descriptions. Leave some description to the imagination.

9. Write a case history of your main characters. Don't let them appear on earth the day the book opens. Give them backgrounds.
10. Keep your characters in character, but allow them to grow as individuals.
11. Be certain your characters are true to their time period and environment.
12. When choosing names for your characters, avoid using similar sounds and avoid using the same first letter. Save longer or foreign-sounding names for functional characters. Make certain the name is appropriate for the time period and the geographical location.
13. Always give your characters a sense of purpose in life, even if it is simply to survive.
14. In order to make your characters believable, give them the proper balance between positive and negative personality traits.
15. To make them sympathetic, give them a problem to which the reader can relate.
16. Avoid cliché characters by giving them some personal trait that sets them apart from similar characters.
17. When you have writer's block, try writing everything you know about your major characters.

Exercise

Take this situation and see how your heroine or hero would behave, taking into consideration background and character.

She was lost. The woods rose up around her like an encroaching wall that threatened to smother her. If she remained in one place, there was a chance she might be found. If she set out on her own without delay, she might find help before time ran out.

6

How to Write
Believable Dialogue

One of the blessings of being writers is that we have an abundance of natural resources all around us. Everyone we meet is a potential character, and every place we go is a potential setting. But these assets can pay off only if we use them. Along with our writing skills, we must develop our powers of observation as well as a habit of writing things down when they occur to us.

Characters and dialogue are created out of composites, bits of information drawn from a myriad of sources, then sifted and distilled until the writer extracts the perfect combination.

Writing dialogue is a necessary skill because most editors look for the white spaces in a manuscript. If there is too little white space, it means that the writer has used too little dialogue, too much narration. When you analyze published novels, note the balance between narration, dialogue and introspection. Young adult novels, in particular, place heavy emphasis on dialogue.

If you learn nothing else about writing dialogue, remember this rule: *Dialogue must not be used without a reason. It must accomplish a specific purpose.*

How can you decide when to write dialogue instead of narration? Here are eleven good reasons for using dialogue:

1. Use Dialogue to Show Characterization
One of the key elements of good characterization is to show contrast between characters. Through dialogue, we give each character his or her own voice and manner of speaking. You should be able to lift unattributed dialogue (dialogue where the name of a speaker is not

designated) at random from your manuscript and still be able to tell who is talking.

In dialogue, characters show us how they think, act, and relate to other characters or events. By doing so, they tell us more about themselves in a few words than the writer could indicate in a page of narration. Through dialogue we can illustrate such qualities as ethnic group, nationality, level of education, gender and, of course, mood or disposition.

One of the easiest ways to show contrast between characters is to use characters with different levels of education. Study the following scene between a schoolteacher and a backwoods trapper.

> "Me I can't see no good reason why I should sign them papers, Miz Cooper. I don't take with givin' out my name lessen there's a powerful big need."
>
> "Of course, Mr. Becker, I understand your position. However the rules are set. There is no way that Polly can attend school unless she has your signed permission."
>
> "Shoot. That's no skin off a hog's back. Poll can keep house for me and look after the younguns, like always."

To set the stage for a teenage novel, writers today have to edit carefully. Four-letter words are becoming a part of everday conversation, but you must carefully assess whether profanity is appropriate for your market. In most cases, it is not. If you are writing for the Christian romance lines you must be even more aware of content.

Yvonne Lehman, in her young adult novel, *Picture Perfect* (Bethany House Publishers), includes dialogue in the opening scene.

> Natalie Ainsworth had been waiting all evening for just the right moment to spring the news.
>
> Now was definitely not the right moment.
>
> "Can you believe that score? Three to ze-rooow—zilch—zip!" screeched Stick Gorden, flopping into a booth at the Pizza Palace.
>
> "Well scoot over, dork!" demanded Ruthie Ryan, her riot of red curls springing around her face. "The rest of us want to sit, too. That is what you're doing, I take it?"

In Myrna Temte's *A Lawman for Kelly* (Silhouette Special Edition #1075), Steve Anderson, a deputy U.S. marshal, often shows his irritation by cursing. It is appropriate for this type of hard-driven character, and so it seems perfectly normal. A ranch setting usually reflects dialogue that is more earthy than you would expect from scenes in an upscale metroplitan setting.

It's as natural for some persons to swear as it is for them to breathe. They swear more out of habit than from irritation. Because many romance readers find swear words distasteful, it is best to use profanity with care. The novice writer is inclined to overdo the use of swear words to the point that they lose their punch. Four-letter words are rarely used in romances. *Hell* and *damn* may be "tastefully" used with some romance lines; however, they are rarely combined with the name of the deity. It is good advice to limit swearing to one character, but that depends on the plot.

If you want to show strong feelings but prefer not to spell out the swear words, easy solutions exist. "He swore competently," "he swore under his breath" and "he cut loose with some words she had never heard before" are all cliché expressions, but they are viable alternatives to including actual swear words.

Dialect, accent or colloquialisms can designate a character's origin. Slang and other buzzwords can indicate a person's profession or lifestyle. Politicians have their own jargon, engineers may speak in computerese, policemen have their street language (it differs from one part of the country to another), and blue-collar workers have their own manner of speaking. Show me a teenager, and I'll show you a language that is almost indecipherable. Here is a conversation I overheard between two girls in a department store.

> "He goes, 'After the dance we can go over to my place.' And I go, 'Over to your place, no way!' And he goes, 'Then let's go over to your place,' and I go, 'We can't go over to my place because you know my dad goes crazy.' Then he laughs and goes, 'Fer sure.' So him and me, we rap for a while and then, he just goes. I was like, bummed out. You know?"

Use slang words and buzzwords sparingly and be careful not to use terms or words that will become dated, unless your purpose is to establish the book in a specific time period.

For the Regency time period one might write: "He was high in the pockets and long in the tooth." Modern slang would translate it to read: "He was broke and over the hill."

Speech mannerisms are verbal tags that can effectively set one character apart from the others. Examples of verbal mannerisms might be the person who constantly interrupts, the person who intersperses dialogue with nonwords such as *um* and *uh*, and the person who stutters.

If you want to *show* without *telling* that a person has low self-esteem, you might use word packages such as: "I may be wrong but . . ." or "this is just my opinion, but . . ." or "you know more about this than I do but . . ."

Be cautious with mannerisms. They can become tiresome to read when overused. Strive for the flavor of the verbal trait instead of the overdose. Even though your character drops the *h* on every word, it is not necessary to write it to that extreme. If the writer drops one *h* in every sentence, the reader will understand that the character speaks with an accent.

Northern writers can be spotted immediately when they try to designate a Southern accent by using the term *you all*. In the first place, Southerners say *y'all*, but that is only one element of a Southern accent. To get the feeling for a regional accent, listen to talk shows or dramas set in the South or read novels by well-known Southern authors. Textbooks on dialect are helpful. See the reference section in the back of this book for a list.

Visual mannerisms that go along with dialogue are also a marvelous tool for characterization. Some examples are: the person who furtively averts his gaze when speaking, the person who punctuates dialogue with hand gestures, the person who speaks with his mouth full, the person who keeps moving closer with each sentence, the person who touches the one to whom he is speaking. Remember that Europeans stand closer together than Americans do while in conversation.

There are dozens of ways to show characterization using the speaker's body language. When you choose a mannerism, use it only for that character so that it will become an identifying tag. Make it appropriate to the character and his lifestyle:

> Jason rocked back on the heels of his boots and regarded her with wry humor. "Lady, don't even try to lie to me. I know you as well as I know my own face."

Rocking back on his heels would be more appropriate for a cowboy or a blue-collar person than for the corporate genius who might have a tag such as this: "He punctuated his words with repeated clicks of his ballpoint pen." Or: "He patted his jacket pockets, looking for the pen he habitually misplaced."

Be careful to show contrast between male and female dialogue. Some writers believe that women tend to speak out of emotion where men speak in terms of action. Also, men are usually more precise. How many times have you heard a man correct a woman who is telling a story? The woman might say the book cost about thirty dollars. The man would say, "Well, actually it was just under twenty-eight. Twenty-seven dollars and ninety-nine cents, plus tax, to be exact."

Word choices also differ for men and women. The best way to learn the proper tone or voice for your character is to develop a listening ear and take notes.

2. Use Dialogue to Give a Sense of Time and Place

If you write both contemporary and historical romances, you will first have to learn to deal with the difference in the tone of the dialogue. Modern language is less formal. We have not only shortcut food, but shortcut language. We use partial sentences, contractions and made-up words.

For example, historical dialogue might read this way: "Indeed! I would not presume to question him on the subject." The contemporary variation might read: "I'm not about to ask him how it happened." Or "No way am I going to open up that can of worms."

Historical dialogue has its slang and contrast between the educated and uneducated person, but it must be consistent with the time period and culture and the national origin of the speaker. To find out if a word was in usage during a specific time period, one reference source is *Merriam-Webster's Collegiate Dictionary*, Tenth Edition. There are other sources but this one is easy to find.

Foreign words and phrases add color and a sense of setting to conversation but, used improperly, they are irritating and a put-down to the reader who does not understand the language.

Notice how Roberta Gellis handles language in *The English Heiress* (Dell, Book Creations).

"Grand-mere," the boy exclaimed, "qu'est-ce que c'est que—"
"Speak English," Roger St. Eyre interrupted. There was no particular expression in his voice, but his step-mother, Lady Margaret,

glanced briefly in his direction before she turned her attention to Phillip who was obligingly repeating in English his question about what had disturbed his grandfather.

Handy language books for travelers are a quick reference for ordinary greetings and remarks. Many large dictionaries have a section devoted to common words and phrases in foreign languages.

3. Use Dialogue to Set the Mood or Tone

Long flowing sentences create conversational, relaxed, sensual moods. Conversation between two people can set up a love scene, but remember, once the excitement begins to build, dialogue should be minimized.

The same holds true for a fast-paced action scene. Put yourself into the scene. Imagine yourself running or walking up a very steep hill. Now picture yourself trying to carry on a long, involved dialogue. The exchanges would be short, concise and to the point.

Wrong

They ran at top speed through the darkened tunnel.

"You have to keep up with me, Maggie, because we've got to get to the bank before they can withdraw the money."

Better

They ran at top speed through the darkened tunnel.

"Run, Maggie, run!" He gulped huge quantities of air that seared his lungs. "We've got to make it. If they get the money first . . ."

We can assume that Maggie knew the consequences. The shorter, incomplete bursts of dialogue add a sense of immediacy and are more believable, coming from a speaker who is running out of breath.

4. Use Dialogue to Inject Humor

Writers who attend conferences hear one message repeated by most editors: "Yes, I love humor in romance novels but not if it is forced."

For many authors humor is difficult. One of the things to avoid is slapstick comedy. The most salable humor is a sort of sophisticated repartee between the hero and heroine. The characters don't have to know that it's funny. They could be caught up in the passion of an argument, but to the reader, who knows that their verbal sparring match is an outward symbol of their sexual frustration, the scene can be amusing.

Avoid editorializing. If you have to tell the reader that the heroine laughed so hard she nearly fell off her chair, something is missing in the humor. The reader should find the dialogue funny, even if the heroine remains glassy eyed and unsmiling.

Stella Cameron's historical romance novel, *Dear Stranger* (Warner Books), will keep you in stitches if you enjoy double entendres and spicy dialogue.

Her book opens with a scene between Lily and her friend, who are spying on a man outside in the churchyard.

> "Well," Lily said, deciding not to mention using her Bible as a stepping stool again. "You have not answered me. The question is, do all men have mysterious parts?"
>
> Rosemary mumbled so low, Lily couldn't understand a word. "Speak up," she said, aware of her sharpness, but not especially contrite.
>
> "I said," Rosemary responded with more than her customary quiet vinegar, "that I'm moved to believe they all do. After all, why should one man be different from another in that respect?"
>
> Lily considered. "Oh, I imagine that even while possessing similar arrangements, they probably are not created exactly the same. But we are agreed that they are all at least similarly burdened. That is something."
>
> "Yes," Rosemary agreed. "Something."
>
> "So one could choose any man to study. Or a number of them, in order to make comparisons."
>
> (then a few paragraphs later)
>
> "We cannot assume that a man's interesting face is an assurance of interesting other things. Why he may be endowed with nothing of note for our purpose."

Oliver Worth, the hero, later becomes the source for Lily's research, much to his consternation . . . and utter delight.

A contemporary novel that exemplifies humorous repartee in series romance is *Right Chest, Wrong Name* by Colleen Collins (Harlequin Love & Laughter). The story involves the hero, who attends a bachelor party before his wedding and is given a tattoo on his chest. Problem is, the name tattooed was Liz. Not the name of his very proper fiancée, Charlotte.

5. Use Dialogue to Slow or Speed Up the Pace

The things characters say can bring them together or move them apart. Most misunderstandings between the hero and heroine can be cleared up by means of a short discussion. Conversely, a discussion where the wrong things are said, or the things said are taken in the wrong way, can effectively delay the decision to make a commitment.

> "There's something I've been wanting to say to you, Ellen."
>
> She waited, seeing the warmth in his eyes and the way his breath came in short, nervous puffs. This was it. He was going to ask her to marry him.
>
> He leaned close and rested his arm across the seat behind her. "I'm crazy about you, Ellen, and I think you feel the same way. Isn't it time we moved in together?"
>
> Ellen blinked. "I don't know, Steve. Is . . . is it marriage we're talking about here?"
>
> "Marriage?" He laughed but the humor failed to reach his eyes. "Marriage is a word that doesn't compute. I was talking about living together."

If Ellen were ready for marriage but not just a relationship, chances are it would take several more chapters to resolve their differences. The differences, or conflict, would provide momentum for the plot even though the actual relationship was losing ground. The hindrance, easily accomplished through the use of dialogue, was stronger than it would have been through narration as shown in the following example:

> Ellen knew from the warmth in his eyes and the way his breath came in short, nervous gasps that Steve had something on his mind. He was as crazy about her as she was about him. The time was right. He was going to ask her to marry him.
>
> He leaned close, resting his arm across the seat behind her. The next thing Ellen knew he was suggesting they share an apartment. Confused, she asked him if he were proposing.
>
> He laughed at that, but his laughter didn't reach his eyes. He told her that he wasn't ready for marriage, but he was willing to share an apartment.

In the second example, we lose immediacy in the telling. It is better to *show*, through dialogue. We want the reader to see and to feel, to be right there on stage where the action is taking place.

6. Use Dialogue to Disseminate Information

Dialogue is an unbeatable tool for planting clues without making it too obvious, for bringing in the family background as well as facts about the immediate characters. It enables the writer to keep the reader on the scene, rather than telling the reader what happened through long paragraphs of passive narration.

Wrong

It took a lot of coaxing for Todd to persuade Jessica to tell him about her ex-fiancé. When she finally did, Todd could see why she had called off the engagement. Michael was the kind of man who would never leave his family. Every decision he ever made had to be cleared with his mother. If she disagreed, there was no recourse, no discussion. Her word was law.

Better

Todd took her hands between his palms. "Look, Jessica. We can't have this wall between us. I have to know about Michael."

Jessica was strengthened by the steady pressure of his hands. Todd was right. If she was ever to get on with her life . . . her voice was surprisingly steady.

"Michael has never learned to make his own decisions. His mother controls him. No matter what it is he wants to do, he always asks her permission." Jessica's eyes clouded for a moment, then cleared. "If I had stayed with him she would have taken over my life, too. I had to end it."

Little gems of information increase momentum. Too much information at one time reminds readers that you are bringing them up to date. As a result, momentum is lost.

7. Use Dialogue to Tighten and Shorten

Think *immediacy*. Long passages of narration can be deleted by putting the characters on stage and rewriting the scene in dialogue. Drama is created out of emotion and conflict. It is only by having our characters in a position where they can react to each other that we can provide that necessary element of drama. Dialogue makes the story active instead of passive, thereby making it stronger and fast paced.

8. Use Dialogue as an Opening Hook

A sure way to spark some editor's interest is to use dialogue to begin chapter one, but it must be dialogue that will grab the reader and hold her until she reaches for her checkbook. Here are a few interesting first chapter openers.

"Don't disappoint me, Emily." *Silver Tomorrows*, Susan Plunkett (Jove Time Passages)

"How curious." *A Garden Folly*, Candice Hern (Signet Regency Romance)

"You will not go! I forbid it!" *Larkspur*, Dorothy Garlock (Warner Books/Historical Romance)

Or: "What do you mean, I'm fired?"

Or: "It's over, Jim. There's only one thing I want from you."

Or: "I knew the minute I came up the walk that something was going on in here."

Or: "Hello, Mason. I'd like you to meet your son."

Most readers would be hooked after reading any of these openings. The idea is to start the imagination working by asking what kind of people they are. Why did the woman lose her job? Was it sexual harassment or was she being replaced by a younger, more attractive woman? What does the speaker want from Jim? What was going on in the room? Didn't Mason know he had a son? Why not? Had he been away . . . or is the woman trying to put something over on him?

Dialogue makes a powerful opening hook but special care must be taken to thoroughly identify the speaker and the reason for the speech before proceeding too far into the book.

Here is one way to establish character as well as the critical situation immediately after the opening line of dialogue.

"You didn't tell me you invited Tod up to the cabin this weekend." Tracey confronted her mother with a look that left no doubt of her anger.

"Really, Tracey," Helen Martin lifted a casserole dish from the cooler. "Tod is your brother. I could hardly avoid asking him for the holidays. Besides, it's time the two of you learned to get along. You've always been such a . . ." She smiled. "Well you know." She waved a hand in dismissal.

Tracey opened her mouth to protest but thought better of it. What good would it do? Tod was the trophy their mother had always wanted to claim. The best musician, the best in sports and always boyishly charming. He knew how to handle their mother. He flirted outrageously with her in front of people until she giggled like a schoolgirl with her first crush.

Tracey, on the other hand, made her mother feel old, threatened. It had been that way since the day that Tracey became a woman. Everything changed then and Tod quickly learned to take advantage.

In just a few words you can show strong characterization immediately after the book opens. Notice how the variation in the length of sentences helps to create mood and character.

9. Use Dialogue as a Transition Bridge

For transition of time:

> Sandy was caught up in the memory of how it had been when she was with Trace. His hands—
>
> "Sandy! This is the third time I called you." Her mother's voice brought her back with a jolt.

For transition of emotions: Dialogue is an acceptable device if you need a sudden change of mood for your characters.

> Karen wasn't sure she had heard him right. "What do you mean, you have three children by a previous marriage?"

> "The job is yours if you want it." He studied her face, waiting for the reaction he knew must come. "There's just one small problem. You'll have to move to Tokyo."

10. Use Dialogue to Break Up Long Passages

Pacing is necessary because many readers have short interest spans. Too much dialogue, narration or introspection is like following the white line on a highway at night—it's hypnotic and can put one to sleep. By breaking up narration or introspection with dialogue, we give the reader a mental jolt that signals twists and turns ahead.

11. Use Dialogue to Show Instead of Tell

Even experienced writers sometimes need to be reminded not to tell the reader what is happening, but to show the action as it unfolds. Verbally illustrating a scene allows the characters emotions to have reasonance and pulls the reader into the conflict.

Wrong

It was one morning in October when she told him she was expecting his child. At first he stared at her as if the early frost had numbed his tongue, then he swallowed hard and told her in a tight voice that he would give her half of the money to pay for the abortion. Otherwise, he knew a couple who would be willing to take on a new baby.

Better

It was one morning in October when she told him she was expecting his child. At first he stared at her as if the early frost had numbed his tongue, then he swallowed and spoke in a tight voice.

"I'm sorry, honey. It must have been that night at the cabin. But don't you worry. I'll help pay for the abortion."

He apparently recognized the disgust written on her face because he shivered once and shoved his hands in his pockets. "Well, if you can't handle that, I guess I know a couple who'd be willing to take on a new baby."

The second example puts the reader right into the scene as it takes place.

Things to Avoid When Writing Dialogue
Avoid Static Dialogue

Or how to say nothing in twenty-five words or more. Think about your telephone calls. The first few minutes are usually devoted to polite exchanges. "Hello. How are you? How is your family?" Other scintillating comments about the weather routinely follow. In novels, we can't give the reader a chance to slip away from us. Instead, we say something like this:

When Peter called Ashley they talked for a few minutes before he brought up the subject of the trip to Seattle. "I hate to tell you this, Ashley, but we have to postpone the trip."

If they meet on the street or in another public place, cut the dialogue to basic essentials:

He was already at the restaurant when she arrived. They found a booth near the door and Peter propped his elbows on the table. "All right. Let's hear all about it. Just start with the day the papers were served."

Avoid Fragmented Exchanges

Wrong

"Listen, Ashley. I have to know now, tonight. Are you going to give me the controlling interest in the company?"

Ashley folded her hands carefully in her lap. There was an intensity in his gaze that confused her. Why was he determined to become the major shareholder? Was it the company or was it her he wanted to control? She desperately needed to talk to her attorney.

"I don't think so, Steve. I need time to make a decision."

Better

"Listen, Ashley, I have to know now, tonight. Are you going to give me the controlling interest in the company?"

Ashley folded her hands carefully in her lap. "I . . . I don't think so, Steve." She was confused by the intensity in his gaze.

"I need time to think before I decide. I need to talk to my attorney." She noticed his clenched hands and wondered why he was so determined to become the major shareholder. Was it the company or was it her he wanted to control?

The object of avoiding fragmented dialogue is to get a response to the dialogue before the reader forgets the question and has to backtrack.

Avoid Forecasting

Don't lose the effect of dialogue by telegraphing ahead.

Wrong

She saw his anger but it only served to strengthen her determination to keep the business in her name. "I'm sorry, Steve. I'm just not ready to give up my control of the corporation."

Better

His anger was obvious from the grim set of his mouth to the way he clenched his fists. She gripped the chair for support. "I'm sorry, Steve. I'm just not ready to give up my control of the corporation."

Wrong

Carolyn discovered James searching through a trunk in the attic. He looked up. "I've been going through the stuff in this old trunk and you'll never guess what I found."

Better

It was in the attic where Carolyn finally found him.

James looked up. "I've been going through the stuff in this old trunk and you'll never guess what I found."

Avoid Unattributed Dialogue

We know that in dialogue each speaker must have a separate paragraph. If there are two speakers in the room, it is not always necessary to include speaker tags—but care must be taken when there is extensive conversation between the two characters reminding the reader whose turn it is to speak. This can be done through body language (action or emotion) or by attribution (he said, she added, he spoke angrily and countless other phrases). Always remember that *said* is usually preferred.

Avoid Redundancy

Wrong

Sharon tossed the stack of papers through the open window. "That's what I think of your offer," she said.

Better

Sharon tossed the stack of papers through the open window. "That's what I think of your offer." (*She said* is redundant.)

Avoid Contortions

Wrong

"I wish you could see how you look in that wig," Carolyn laughed.

To correct: There should be a period after *wig*, instead of a comma. You cannot laugh sentences. If the sentence had read *Carolyn said* instead of *Carolyn laughed*, then the first punctuation would have been acceptable.

Do not use quotation marks for internal dialogue. If you want a word or phrase to be in italics, underline the passage in your manuscript. Use it sparingly. Never, never capitalize all the letters in a word for emphasis. They only do that in porn novels, so I'm told.

When you have completed the first draft of a passage of dialogue, read it aloud; better yet, read it into a tape recorder. Hearing it instead of seeing it can reveal a multitude of flaws. Dialogue must have a purpose and must flow naturally through the individual voices of your characters while the writer remains in the background as liaison between character and reader. To achieve this, we must first know how our characters will respond to a given set of circumstances. That's when your characters come alive. That's when you get a phone call from an editor, saying that she loves your book and is ready to go to contract. And that has to be the greatest dialogue of all.

Exercises

Make television your tool. Listen to the sound without watching the picture. Imagine what the speakers are doing. Listen for the breath patterns. Listen for the silences. Writer and teacher Madeline DiMaggio reminds her students that silences are extremely powerful. Listen for the pauses that add punch to the dialogue. Then turn off the sound and watch the picture. Study the body movements and the facial expressions. Note the use of hands during a conversation.

Dialogue Checklist

1. Does each line of dialogue have a purpose, fill some function?
2. Does the conversation sound natural, or is it stilted?
3. Is the dialogue appropriate to the time period, to the characters and to the locale?
4. Does it flow well?
5. Does the pace relate to the action? Long sentences for a slow pace, short sentences to reflect action, tension or suspense?
6. Does each passage of dialogue lead into the next?

7. Is there a proper balance between narration, dialogue and internal monologue?
8. Is the speaker easily identified?
9. Do you show contrast between speakers? Does each character have his or her own voice? Is the dialogue true to the character?
10. Have you broken up long passages of dialogue with action or narration?
11. Have you punctuated correctly?
12. Have you used dialect or foreign words too frequently?
13. Is the humor overdone?
14. Have you told too much and left nothing to the imagination?
15. Does the dialogue move the story forward or is some of the dialogue too mundane?
16. Does the dialogue sparkle?

7

Setting and Background

*I*n a romance novel, everything must take second place to the relationship between the hero and heroine. To make that relationship believable, we must provide a stage on which the romance takes place. This arena of action can be a real place or an imaginary setting, but it must come alive to the reader, enabling her to "be there" without ever having actually visited. By providing the reader with an appropriate setting, we build a foundation for the characters, mood and action. Perhaps most important of all, we supply one more channel to reader identification.

How often have you read a book and remembered having dinner in a restaurant the writer described or flying into a particular airport, taking a cable car, or riding that same glass elevator detailed in the story? Place recognition through the use of real names of real places transports the reader into the scene right along with the characters.

The Importance of Specifics

It is important to deal with specifics instead of abstracts. When describing houses, don't say that houses were clustered at the foot of the hill. Instead, describe weathered houses with their paint dulled to a mauve patina or freshly painted houses of every design, from A-frame to quaint Dutch colonial architecture. Wild animals do not roam the hills. Elk, deer and the occasional cougar hunt the sparsely wooded hills where wild huckleberries grow in profusion.

In my book *Midsummer Madness*, part of the cover-up involved the mayor and city council of the town where the story was set. Instead of using the name of a real town, I made up a name but centered details of the plot amid several towns that actually do exist. Using the names of well-known streets and freeways provided enough authenticity that a reader who was familiar with the area knew exactly where the town was located. Threads of reality woven into the structure of fiction help to make it ring true.

In some novels, maps are included at the front of the book to identify the locale as a real place or as an imaginary place set amidst real landmarks. A disclaimer is used to indicate fictional sites. This device is beneficial to the reader, who can follow the action in the story by using the map as reference.

Choose Your Setting Carefully

Some editorial guidelines impose certain restrictions on the choice of setting. Harlequin Romances may take place "anywhere in the world as long as there is some romantic atmosphere conveyed." An exotic setting is desirable, but only if it is described naturally and blended with the plot, not fitted into the story like copy from a traveler's guidebook! As one editor said at a Romance Writers of America conference, "We like the setting worked naturally into the story. For example, they're drifting down the Thames. Don't be a tour guide. We prefer the hero humming in her ear, 'Here comes the bloody tower.' "

Harlequin Presents has similar requirements, except for the preference of the exotic element."The setting must be romantic and integral to the mood the author creates."

Four words illustrate Harlequin American Romance novels: contemporary, realistic, mature, American. They capture the flavor of what it's like to live in America.

Because a great number of writers live in California and Texas, many romance novelists use those settings for their books. Editors suggest that writers select less familiar places whenever possible. Just as publishers try not to publish successive books with similar plots or with the protagonists having similar careers, editors try to vary the settings.

But again, discretion must be used. Least likely to succeed are settings such as Africa, the Middle East, Russia, India or Cuba. Use caution when setting your story in any country that might be considered too poverty stricken to provide a romantic setting, or too involved in political upheaval to offer a sympathetic background.

Although some editorial guidelines suggest that books be set in "exotic locations," many books are set in average, middle-class surroundings. An exotic location may be a bigger-than-life setting such as a castle on the Rhine or any place that has a touch of the extraordinary. For most romance lines, a coal-mining town would not fit the description, nor would a poor area of a backward country; it is too difficult to imagine these as romantic settings. A small-town setting with a fashionable resort, an Olympic-trial ski run or other point of interest could easily be considered exotic.

Editors insist that any setting used in a book must be described with complete accuracy and believability. The logical approach is to simplify your research by writing about where you live. Try to see your own setting as if you were visiting it for the first time. What do you find appealing about it? Romantic? Exotic? Study the past history of your town, keeping in mind that background is as important to place as it is to a character.

If your plot dictates a more remote setting, don't panic. As someone once said, "It is not necessary to break an arm to know that it hurts." A writer can learn enough about a place to use it as a setting without ever having been there. Study the chapter on research to discover how it's done. A few carefully selected bits of information can give the flavor of authenticity necessary in setting the stage for romance.

The details we choose are the lifeblood of our fiction. A setting should not be chosen at random but should interact with the characters. Setting can even be used as a tool for characterization. How a person lives can clearly reflect his or her personality. A yard full of weeds, shutters hanging at half-mast and newspapers strewn around the room denotes one kind of character while an orderly, well-kept house gives evidence of another kind of personality.

The setting should also contribute to the developing romance. Too often beginning writers neglect the use of senses when setting up a love scene. Think of your first romantic kiss. Visualize the setting. Chances are it will be easier to recall than the face of your first love. Years later, the scent of pine needles, the lap of water against the sand, or the headiness of a fading gardenia may trigger an emotional response that instantly zaps you back to that one special moment in time.

Sensual tags such as these can be used in introspection to trigger a "come-to-realize" scene:

Kristin was drawn to the garden by the fragrance of mint drifting on the evening breeze. Memories came flooding back until she felt as if she were drowning in them. Memories of the afternoon they had picnicked here in the herb garden. Memories of James and the way his lips brushed her face. The scent of crushed mint mingled with the faint spice of his after-shave was indelibly etched into her senses, reminding her always of the day he said he loved her. Being here again was like being in his arms. She had been wrong about him. She missed him, wanted him. She had to find him now. Before it was too late.

Authors commonly make two serious mistakes when they create settings. Once research is begun, there is such a wealth of material to be found that it seems a shame to waste it. Then, to compound the mistake, authors dump all the information on the reader at one time. The result is a geography lesson rather than a story. The plot loses momentum—and the author loses the reader.

Wrong

Michael helped Jillian out of the car and motioned to the wide walkway. "These steps lead to the verandah that was built after the mansion was partly destroyed by fire in 1822. That was when Aaron Marsden lived here with his aging mother. They say there were five stairways in the house, but only three of them have been discovered." He pointed to the tall pillars which stood at the entrance rotunda. "The columns are forty-feet tall and are made of inlaid mahogany, cypress, and ivory with rosewood terminals."

Although this information may be important to the story, there is no interaction with the characters, and the reader is sure to feel that she is being lectured to. It would have been better to let Jillian see the leaded window facing the garden where the woman once sat in her wheelchair, and for her to feel the smooth parquetry of the inlaid pillars, and to hear her heels click on the walkway leading to the verandah.

The least intrusive way to filter in background information is to let the reader see the setting through the character's eyes. Here's an example from *The Scout's Bride* by Kate Kingsley (Harlequin Historical #354). The setting is Fort Chamberlain, a cavalry hospital where Rebecca is helping care for soldiers who survived a battle with Native Americans.

In the operating room Rebecca removed the sheets from the two tables in its center. Though she had prepared the room several times, she could hardly bear to look at the larger table, gouged and scratched, stained with blood that could not be scrubbed away. . . .

(a paragraph or two later)

Waiting for boiling water from the kitchen, she filled the lanterns and trimmed the wicks. She saw there was a pitcher of clean water on the washstand, then reluctantly gathered the surgical tools from the cabinet: scalpel, lancet, saw, even a small hammer and chisel.

When a nurse delivered a steaming kettle, Rebecca placed the instruments in a deep pan and poured scalding water over them. While they soaked, she scoured the tables with hard, yellow, army-issue soap, sluicing the excess water onto the floor. The puddles evaporated almost immediately in the dry heat.

In her reluctance to look at the table, we sense Rebecca's dread over what is about to happen. We get the feeling that she is working quickly, automatically, so as not to have to think about it. The scene is strong because of the obvious as well as the implied emotion.

A sense of personal awareness is vital. When dialogue is used to describe a setting, it could be mixed with introspection to punch up the emotional impact.

In Diana Whitney's novel, *A Hero's Child* (Silhouette Special Edition #1090), the heroine, Rae Hooper, has agonized over the renovations that will save her hometown by making it a tourist attraction.

Rae moistened her lips and spoke in a firm voice that only shook a little. "When my grandmother opened this diner, talking pictures were considered a fad, flappers raised eyebrows with their bare knees and bobbed hair, and back room speakeasies got rich on bathtub booze."

Ann Maxwell uses characterization techniques for the setting as well as the people. She says: "I also use the same technique when describing place; such descriptions are also metaphor for character and relationship."

In Gothic novels the setting is as much a part of the story as are the characters and must, like the characters, be thoroughly delineated. Gothics are "mood pieces," which revolve primarily around the heroine's feeling that she or someone close to her is in jeopardy. They may contain an element of romance, depending on the publisher.

> She had searched for it before, the old house lost somewhere amidst the trees and giant ferns of the cypress swamp. But it had always eluded her as if it were indeed a figment of a childhood dream. This time, this time she would find it. It was close now, watching her. She felt its breath, damp and fetid against her bare arm, even as the forest drew close around her. And then it was there. It rose up in front of her, old and weathered, ugly as a vulture astride day-old carrion. The paint had chipped away in most places but here and there in tiny cracks and slivered crevices, the house bled. It was the Red house. The place where she died and was reborn.

Phyllis Whitney and Victoria Holt are the acknowledged experts at creating a Gothic mood or tone out of setting. If Gothics interest you, you might enquire into *The Gothic Journal*, a newsletter for writers. You will find the address in the list of resources at the back of this book.

The choice of setting and location should be appropriate to the story and the character. Romance can be found in most places, but some places seem to be made just for lovers.

> The drive up from the storm littered beach was a short one. Lettie was not prepared for the profusion of flowers and shrubs. To the left she glimpsed graceful colonades with marble staircases leading to a Greco-Roman temple. A succession of shaded walkways twisted and turned through formal gardens enhanced with statues of Greek heroes. She did a double take. Someone had brushed bright pink paint on the statues' male appendages.

Setting or background provides an ideal device for motivation. A character can be motivated to fear dark places if that character had been locked in a dark cellar as a child. The setting in *Gone With The Wind*, the plantation Tara at the end of the Civil War provides the motivation for most of the conflict. Everything Scarlett does is directed by her efforts to save her plantation.

Readers never seem to get enough stories about cowboys and ranches, whether they are set in contemporary or historical times. The locale is crucial to the plot, as are the heroes who may be gritty or urbane or a combination of both. Outdoor settings are frequently used because they lend themselves well to romantic adventures, danger, conflict and a sense of splendid isolation.

Research is important to add credibility. Don't plant birch trees in Colorado if they aren't native to the climate. *Rawhide and Lace,* a newsletter for the western aficionada, is a fine source of reference and information for the western writer. Look for the address in the back of this book.

Scents, sounds, the texture of a place, the tempo, the lightness or heaviness of the air, the presence of personal belongings in a room, the presence or lack of order, lighting and humidity are just a few elements of setting that contribute substance and texture to a novel.

Because places make such strong, subliminal impressions, we can, through careful planning and delineation of settings, take a reader back in time. We can increase suspense, sexual tension, mood and motivation. We can make the reader feel that she is there with the characters in the very center of the stage.

Developing the Romantic Plot

8

*A*ny literary work involving upwards of 50,000 words cannot be a random sampling of ideas. A romance novel must be carefully conceived and constructed to hold the reader's interest, to follow a central idea, and to permit the reader to enter an unreal world and find it believable. This is true whether the novel you are writing is contemporary or historical, light romance or sensually explicit.

Debra Matteucci, Senior Editor and Editorial Coordinator of Harlequin Books, says: "A strong plot is an imperative ingredient. Some writers get confused between *plot* and *romance*. The romance is not the plot! There must be some action, some issue, some problem to be worked out during the course of the story—that's the plot: simply the organization of incidents. Beyond the plot—or woven throughout the plot—lies the romance. It builds and changes as do the events about which you are writing."

Plot development is not the same for all novels. The shorter the novel, the less intricate the plot. Lines such as Harlequin Romance and Silhouette Romance are usually straight-line romances without obvious subplots. Longer romances, such as the Harlequin Super-romance, Harlequin American Romance and Loveswept Romance lines have subplots.

Single title and mainstream novels, which are more complex than series novels in both subject levels and length, can have several related or interrelated subplots. Rather than running in a straight line, the story line branches off in many directions.

Even though the plots may evolve in different ways, the important thing to remember in the romance novel is that the characters must come first, and then, out of their lives, their conflicts, their goals, the story is born.

In developing the plot to your novel there are many ways to begin. Each writer eventually finds her own way of working.

Learn to Write a Synopsis

Ann Maxwell says: "I can't think of any advice that is more vital and more often ignored by beginning writers than to write a synopsis. Without it, your story will wander all over, loop about, and ultimately fall far short of what it could have been. Until you know where your story is going, you haven't the faintest idea of the most engrossing, emotionally satisfying way of getting there."

Writing a synopsis is a skill that should be learned early on. Multi-published authors may receive a contract on the basis of a synopsis or a synopsis and sample chapters. Although first-book authors usually must complete the book before receiving a contract, they still need a well-constructed synopsis as a "sales pitch" to woo both editors and agents.

But equally important, the synopsis can tell you whether or not your book will work as a romance novel. I have found that it is much easier to write a synopsis before the book is written. You have only the bare bones of a plot along with the main premise of the story to deal with, instead of a multitude of scenes to consider.

First I establish my characters and their goals, then the premise, and then three or four dramatic or emotional scenes to support the story. Once I have it well in mind, I write a synopsis. When I am ready to actually begin writing, I take the synopsis and break it up into chapters. The first three paragraphs in chapter one, the next two (or four, the numbers vary with each book) paragraphs in chapter two, and so on until I have the required number of chapters in the book. There are always additional scenes that were not spelled out in the synopsis.

While some writers are able to simply "let the story flow," developing the plot as they write, it is very easy for such a novel to fall apart after the first few chapters. Many writers use the synopsis as a guide to maintain the general plot line. Plotting the synopsis is the best way to sustain the energy and momentum of the story while still keeping to the main premise and conflict. Beginners are well advised to save time and frustration by determining the direction of the story before it is written.

Plot vs. Character

At first glance, some might assume the plot to be the most important element in a novel, but most experts agree it is the characters who make the story. If you analyze popular novels, you will soon discover that the most memorable stories are those with strong, believable characters. At the same time, we must realize this: Static characters do not create drama. Characters in action, with or against each other, are an essential part of plotting.

Like most other novels, a romance novel must have a beginning, a middle and an end. To be compelling, a novel must also have the *momentum*, or energy, which comes from a well-constructed plot. Through the creation of strong characters, their conflicts and their motivations, the plot will begin to evolve. Although the developing relationship between the protagonists is of utmost importance, the romance by itself does not constitute the plot.

Plot is a series of connected events in the lives of the characters which provides the action, drama and suspense. Through motivation of our characters, we set up situations or conflicts that are the catalyst for action.

By careful selection of those situations, we create scenes that are relevant, interesting and dramatic. It is the strategic placing of the scenes in our novel that gives vitality to the plot and propels the story forward.

Most romance plots fall into one or more basic patterns of structure or theme. Here are some examples.

Plot Patterns

1. The Ticking Clock: These are plot lines where time is of the essence. The heroine must retrieve the letter before it is found; the poison will prove fatal unless the antidote is administered before a certain time; the protagonists must raise the money to save the historical site before the developers arrive with their bulldozers; the heroine must get back to the time capsule before the hero disappears forever. There are countless combinations of the time element and the romance element that can be used in the romance novel. Keep them fast paced and make use of many obstacles to heighten the tension.

2. The Unsolved Crime: Gothics, intrigues, romantic suspense, historicals—almost any kind of romance novel can make use of this pattern. Step-by-step descriptions are imperative so the reader can participate, be right on stage with the protagonists as they unravel the mystery. Surprise your reader, but never cheat her by giving false information.

3. Developing Relationships: All romance novels focus on the developing relationship between the hero and heroine, but most romance novels have an additional conflict. If your plot deals primarily with the interrelationship of characters, you must delve deeply into the psychology of that relationship, establish unusually strong characters who contrast sharply with one another, and provide logical motivations for that contrast. The conflict must arise from those character differences and must be strong enough to sustain itself throughout the book.

4. Evolution of a Family: Here we look for intense character contrast and growth. Frequently the characters, and often the environment, are pitted against each other. This pattern lends itself well to the big historical novel.

5. Other Worlds/Future Worlds/Time Travel: These elements are now being used in combination with the developing relationship of the romance plot, both contemporary and historical. The setting is of major importance, as is careful attention to details of time and place to provide the feeling of authenticity.

6. Vengeance: This pattern is appropriate for historical or contemporary novels as well as the futuristic novel. Conflict between characters must be strong enough to last throughout the major portion of the book, and it must be believable. Motivation is of prime importance.

7. Personal Struggle/Search for Self: Overcoming tragedy. The writer must have insight into the psychology of the characters to understand how and why they would react to given situations. Motivation must be stressed.

8. Adventure: The movie *Romancing the Stone* is a fine example of this larger-than-life plot pattern. The characters may be both physically and mentally geared for such adventures, or the crux of the plot might be that one or both of the protagonists must learn to cope with the challenges of the adventure. One of my favorites is *African Queen*, where two people who are ill-prepared for a grand adventure succeed, despite their personal frailties and conflicts.

9. Quest: The quest pattern may include such ploys as the search for a lost parent or lost child, a treasure hunt, the determination to save a historical building or any such fixed goal. The key element here is the absolute commitment of the protagonists to succeed in the quest, despite all odds. There should be many obstacles to provide setbacks.

10. Historical Novel/Historical Romance: A plot pattern for the historical novel is based on historical fact, and the plot is determined by those same historical events. Certain portions, such as dialogue, are necessarily fictionalized. The historical romance uses actual events and actual historical characters, but those characters usually play a functional role, merely to help set the stage. Fictionalized characters are the main protagonists. The plots rely heavily on the color and essence of the time to validate the pattern.

11. Survival: Survival plots can be as simple as a woman trying to make it on her own after having been deserted, or as complicated as the struggle to live through a hurricane. This pattern often works in combination with the ticking-clock plot line; for example, a plane wreck in the wilderness where the lives of the survivors depend on finding food or medical care. Again, the setting, obstacles, hindrances and furtherances play a huge part in creating the drama. The tension must build with each successive scene.

12. Social/Society and Civilization/Lifestyles: Gothics, the Regency novel, other historical novels and many contemporary novels can fit into this plot pattern. Although the plot must focus on the characters and their conflicts, you will soon discover the way of life is in itself another character in the developing drama. The Regency novel is an excellent example of how drawing room manners can create a plot line for a book.

13. Power Play/Political Intrigues: This plot centers on one person or group attempting to control another group. Strong characterization is vital to this kind of pattern. The focus of a power-play plot demands a single-minded pursuit of power against all odds. This pattern combines well with the revenge or ticking-clock pattern. In the romance novel, the power play is often depicted as the heroine (a David-like character) taking on the hero (Goliath). The heroine may or may not win the contest, but she always wins the hero. As trends change and heroes often become the main viewpoint protagonist, a story might begin with the hero as David and the heroine as Goliath. The hero would have to prove his strength early on in the book to avoid being seen as a wimp.

There are without doubt other plot patterns and other combinations. The premise of your novel should give you a clue as to which pattern fits. Remember that patterns can be combined for use as part of the central plot or as a separate or interwoven subplot, depending on the length of your novel.

In Lindsay Longford's book that won the Rita award, *Renegade's Redemption* (Silhouette Intimate Moments #769), Elly, a single parent, is on the run from her vengeful ex-husband. The hero, Royal Gaines, is an ex-cop bent on self-destruction. In his determination to protect her, Gaines becomes a changed man, and Elly and her son learn to trust. This story could fit into the ticking-clock pattern as well as the adventure, vengeance and survival patterns.

Susan Plunkett's novel for Jove, *Silver Tomorrows*, is an excellent example of a time travel novel that exemplifies the other-worlds pattern as well as those of survival and quest.

Nora Roberts's *Megan's Mate* (Silhouette Intimate Moments #745) book is the story of a single parent and her struggle to rear her child. In addition to being a survival story, it also fits into the evolution-of-a-family pattern since it is a part of Silhouette's *The Calhoun Saga*.

Reducing a novel to its basic theme or premise takes practice, but if you learn the knack early on, you will find it much easier to stay on track while you write the book.

Check the "Books" supplement in your Sunday paper for the list of bestsellers. It often includes one-liners that suggest the premise of the books on the current list.

The Critical Situation

When you have established your novel's premise, you should determine the critical situation. This is the problem the heroine must face as the book opens—a significant problem that will ultimately change the course of her life. Her set goal often causes or contributes to this problem.

A critical situation could be the first day on a new job, an auto accident, seeing someone from the past, an emotion-packed message, someone asking a favor the heroine is hesitant to grant. It is vital that the situation be within the bounds of believability, so romance readers are able to identify with the problem. The details of critical situation depend on the kind of book you are writing. If the book is a romantic suspense or intrigue novel, the critical situation should present an element of suspense, establishing the mood or tone from the start.

No matter what premise you select, the critical situation should reflect change and lead to the conflict. The sum of the two situations plus a satisfactory resolution should equal a plot that both provides an element of fantasy and lies well within the realm of believability.

A card game leads to the critical situation in *Loving Becky*, a Dell Historical Romance and Diamond Debut Award Winner by Kim Lewis. The Earl of Ruxton, in a futile attempt to cover his gambling losses, jokingly says, "What does a man have to do to gain credit here? Sacrifice his eldest son?"

The local squire, his gambling companion, immediately seizes the opportunity to unload one of his daughters. In-as-much as there are witnesses to the wager, the bet is sealed, and, of course, the earl is the loser and must hand over his son.

The conflict begins when we learn that Becky Tallant had no intention of becoming her father's pawn. Nor did the earl's eldest son, Alex, who was smitten with the lovely young Felicia and already betrothed to her. Alex offers a compromise to save face for the fathers: a year-long betrothal to buy time until a reasonable solution can be found to free them from the debt of honor.

In her book *A Dark and Stormy Night* (Harlequin American Romance #702/More Than Men series), Anne Stuart, a master of mood and intrigue, grabs the reader from the first page and never lets go. O'Neal, the hero, gives the first hint of suspense in the prologue. He is a dark, moody man beset by devils we have yet to meet. Katie Flynn, driving in the midst of a hurricane, is nearly swept off a cliff but is dragged from her car by O'Neal and a hulking young giant only seconds before the car slides over the embankment. And then the tensions in the story build. Katie is given refuge in O'Neal's house, a former mental institution. The immediate danger is painted in a broad stroke when we learn that the deranged giant, the housekeeper's son, has a passion for killing people . . . and his mother lets him! Motives are hidden at the beginning, but there is no doubt in the reader's mind that danger lurks behind every drapery.

A strong critical situation can be a dramatic hook that grabs the reader and flings her headlong into the story. It should appear as close to the beginning of the book as is logically possible.

There is an old but still valid saying in literary circles: "A writer has three pages to hook an editor but only one page to hook a reader." Don't waste those precious pages with pointless narrative. Instead, give your reader something substantial to whet her appetite by creating a compelling critical situation that must be resolved.

Conflict

Having established the critical situation, we must lead the reader into the conflict that brings characters into the arena of action. Conflict equals drama. Without conflict, the story will be lifeless. But conflict must arise out of human situations, such as man (mankind) against man, man against nature, and man against himself.

To narrow it down, conflict is born out of such human characteristics as greed, duty, love, misunderstandings, curiosity, hate, revenge, self-preservation and self-discovery. In choosing a point of conflict, you must avoid using a trait that would be out of character. For example, greed would be hard to justify in a heroine. It could, however, be used very nicely in a subplot for a secondary character.

Multipublished author and columnist, Jo Beverley says: "Conflict, of course, is not intrinsically fighting, though the internal stress plus external pressure can wear temper and patience to a painful nub so that fights ensue. In my book *Forbidden Magic* (Topaz), the heroine's original stress—perilous poverty—is alleviated by marriage to a rich earl. However, he then becomes her stress by the sheer energy and dominance of his charming personality. As a more conservative, thoughtful person, she needs time, lots of time, to grow used to such an abrupt change in her life. She also needs to be in control, which she most definitely isn't.

"I think you can see that there's no bad guy in this scenario, but there is a lot of stress which can, as in life, go either way. Without external stress, these two pleasant and essentially reasonable people would work out their problems quite quickly—and thus have no story. It's the external stress that tears a rift in their lives, exacerbating their mild misalignment."

On the night of her wedding Meg felt reasonably safe in her long, close-fitting robe. She was ready to face her new husband and when he came through the doorway to the adjoining room he wore a long robe the color of a Bengal tiger. Her concern seemed foolish now that she saw him dressed even more modestly than she.

But somehow the thought was unsettling. How dared he?

When he perched on the side of the bed and asked if she would like to talk, his nonchalance annoyed her and she confronted him.

He was amused by her burst of temper and pretended innocence while at the same time, allowing his robe to fall open to reveal his long, sexy legs.

Mcg tried to look away but not before she guessed, and correctly so, that he was completely nude beneath his striped robe. The thought did little to still her racing heart.

As the scene continues, Saxonhurst, or Sax, as he preferred to be called, proceeds to tease and at the same time, infuriate her.

With her typical skill Jo Beverley sets up a delightfully lively and sensual scene without the hint of anger that so many authors use to create conflict. We can clearly see Meg's sense of anticipation, her reluctance to admit it, even to herself, and her frustration when he doesn't demand that she "entertain" him.

In Joanna Wayne's *Family Ties* (Harlequin Intrigue #444), the basic conflict arises out of the fact that Ashley and Dillon broke up on the day of their marriage because of her questionable past. Now that Dillon has discovered he is the father of her secret child, he claims the boy and wants to raise him on his ranch. The villain's pursuit of Ashley in order to find the missing money adds conflict as well.

Secret babies are an extremely common basis for conflict in romance novels because readers like the subject. The true test of a writer's creativity is her ability to invent a plot that has a new twist, keeps moving and is believable.

Jane Peart, author of *The Risk of Loving* for Harlequin's Steeple Hill Love Inspired line, uses the hero's loss of his wife and the mother of his child as a device to make him afraid to fall in love again. Mark, a newspaper columnist, finds himself attracted to Coryn. But after a few dates, he abruptly stops seeing her without explanation. Coryn's father is about to run for political office. Interwoven subplots involve Coryn's mother, who is in the initial stages of Alzheimer's Disease, and the death of Coryn's dog, all neatly tied together to make an inspiring and informative read.

In longer novels, second levels of conflict may occur in subplots. These may be interconnected with the primary conflict, or they may be complete in themselves.

The conflict must not be so easily resolved that it cannot sustain the story throughout the required number of pages. If one conflict is resolved, additional conflicts may be introduced, but they should arise naturally out of the original conflict to maintain continuity.

Subplots

A linear plot line, one that focuses on the development of a single idea or conflict, may well be sufficient for the short novel of 50,000 to 60,000 words. When you expand the novel to greater length, you will discover that the plot must branch off in other directions in order to have enough substance to keep the narrative alive.

At the same time, we must take care that the original premise of the novel, the red thread that stitches the story together, remains the same throughout the book. We must also be aware that it is extremely easy for aggressive secondary characters to take over a subplot to the point that they become more important than the major characters. Neither the subplot nor secondary characters should ever be permitted to overshadow the premise of the novel or the main protagonists.

A subplot may be a *separate but parallel* story involving one or both of the protagonists, or it may be an *interwoven* subplot that involves one or both of the protagonists.

The parallel subplot is one that can be lifted in its entirety from the novel without changing the context of the story. For example, it could be a conflict involving a parent who is being brought up on charges of medical malpractice. The protagonist (the son of the doctor) is emotionally affected by his father's problem but not directly involved.

In the interwoven subplot, the son might be a member of the legal team who is responsible for his father's defense. To remove that portion of the conflict would leave a hole in the plot line and substantially change the direction of the plot.

The strongest subplots are those that arise from the basic conflict, exist on more than one level and cannot be removed from the central plot without changing the focus of the story.

A *second-level subplot* evolves from either a parallel or interwoven primary subplot. In the scenario of the doctor under investigation for medical malpractice, a second-level subplot might be the doctor's failing health or the fact that he doesn't want the case to go to court because he has hidden interests in a group of illegal cancer clinics.

When more than one subplot is used in a novel, the writer may combine both parallel and interwoven subplots. In addition, a subplot may begin on a parallel line, then as the novel evolves, interweave with the primary plot. This is most often true in mystery or suspense novels where the author is attempting to conceal the fact that a minor or functional character is a valid suspect.

This type of subplot is also effective in the saga (generational) novel, where a set of characters, perhaps children, are merely functional characters until something happens (the death of a parent) that brings them into the main plot of the story.

Plot patterns such as airplane disasters that utilize the omniscient viewpoint may have a number of plots held together by a common thread.

To summarize, begin with a problem, a critical situation that forces the heroine or hero to take some action or make a decision that could significantly alter the direction of his or her life. The decision leads to conflict with the hero (or heroine) and/or other people and acts as a catalyst for emotional reactions and drama until all of the conflict (or at least the significant conflict) is finally resolved.

Checklist for Plot

- What is the premise of the novel?
- Does the book begin in the proper place?
- Is the plot line slanted toward a specific market or does it fall between the cracks?
- Does the plot flow smoothly from scene to scene? Is each scene necessary?
- Is the pace guaranteed to hold the reader's interest?
- What makes this plot line different from similar novels? Is the plot strong enough to sustain interest?

- Are the characters strong enough to carry the plot? Are they believable? Sympathetic?
- Do the subplots relate to the main theme? Are they brought to conclusion?
- Is there enough conflict? Is it believable? Does the conflict point to the climax?
- Do all the elements of the plot comprise a satisfying ending?

Forty-Four Critical Situations and Points of Conflict

Following is a list of possible romance novel plots suggested by author/teacher Louise Vernon. Use them singly or combine them with one other plot or more, then fit them into a plot pattern and create your own unique plot.

1. Heroine rescues the hero.
2. He rescues her.
3. She tempts him in order to discover his identity.
4. She tempts him to obtain something he doesn't want to part with.
5. She hates him before she loves him.
6. She's in a predicament, about to be fired. Help comes from an unexpected source—for a price.
7. She has been warned that he is out to destroy her well-earned achievements.
8. She divulges a secret through foolish pride and thus destroys something dear to his heart.
9. Her imprudent curiosity threatens their relationship.
10. She is informed that he is married.
11. He's not really her cousin because she's adopted.
12. She sacrifices her love because of a promise.
13. She sacrifices her love for the sake of a parent's happiness.
14. She gives up a successful career to be with him.
15. She has to give up her child.
16. Two men love her but one is not quite honorable.
17. She suppresses her suspicion for the sake of a cause.
18. She's accused of something she didn't do.
19. Her lover's father believes his son is guilty of something.
20. She asks for help—or seeks help for another person. It is refused. Someone comes and helps.
21. Her sister or cousin loves him, too.

22. Something is taken from her. She seeks justice. (She has been mistakenly accused, for example.)
23. She promised something she now cannot fulfill. She must face the consequences.
24. She makes a mistake. Someone takes revenge on her child.
25. She cannot handle the situation and flees. Someone follows and catches up with her.
26. She sacrificed a great deal. Now her life has no meaning.
27. She trusted him to protect her, but he didn't.
28. She joins a group revolting against oppression.
29. She puts a dangerous plan into effect to win him back.
30. He thinks she's on the streets.
31. Her family doesn't like him.
32. His family doesn't like her.
33. She's headstrong and goes against her own best interests.
34. He's in charge of her life, and she rebels.
35. She finds him again.
36. She has lost him because she would not betray a professional secret.
37. The husband she thought dead returns to complicate her life.
38. The marriage was invalid.
39. The divorce was invalid.
40. He wants children which she cannot have.
41. He is sterile. She wants children.
42. They are in competition for the same thing.
43. They must face a natural disaster.
44. They come from two different worlds.

9
Constructing Scenes

A scene is a unit of continuous related action. Successive scenes provide for a cohesive plot and contribute to effective pacing. Scenes are to writing a novel what a framework is to a skyscraper. In the same way that each level of construction raises a building higher and higher, each scene carries the reader closer to the climax and expands the reader's view or range of focus. A single-scene story would necessarily be short. In order to have a multilevel plot line with significant emotional impact, action and drama, a writer must learn to develop energetic scenes.

In novels, a change of scene can be a change of setting, a change of characters or viewpoint, a change of emotions or a time transition. A rule of thumb is that there are three scenes per chapter and a more dramatic scene or pivotal scene every fifth chapter. Of course this simplified rule cannot apply to every novel, but if you use it as a guide, you will find it much easier to analyze the pace and to make sure you maintain momentum throughout the novel.

Nine Kinds of Scenes
Certain scenes are common to most novels. To fully explore the construction of a scene you must first take into consideration the kind of novel you are writing. It should be noted, however, that certain scenes are mandatory, no matter what kind of fiction you are writing. In a romance novel, there are nine types of scenes.

1. The Opening Scene
This scene appears within the first few paragraphs of the novel. It is the *hook* that so intrigues the reader, making it impossible to put the

book down. The opening of a series romance novel is logically much faster than that of a mainstream or single title novel. One of the reasons is that with the shorter length of series novels, the author does not have the freedom to digress. Many authors feel that the first few lines of a novel may well be the most difficult to write.

The protagonist, whether the heroine or the hero, must appear on stage at or near the beginning, followed as soon as possible by the other protagonist. The reason for this is the difficulty in developing a relationship when the characters are apart.

Since about 1984 when the perspective of male viewpoint became acceptable, quite a number of books have begun with the hero's viewpoint. As romance novels have evolved, the hero has been allowed more space to develop into a strong, *believable* character with feelings and motivations, instead of merely presenting the image of an arrogant protector.

In Diana Whitney's series novel *A Hero's Child* (Silhouette Special Edition #1090), the book opens with a road-weary hitchhiker catching a ride to the small town of Gold River. We are fully aware that he is reluctant to continue his journey, but something drives him to go forward. Then the story jumps to the heroine's viewpoint where we learn that her husband walked out on her several years ago. The heroine has a daughter. The reader senses immediately that the hero knows nothing about the child. The critical situation, with the impending meeting of hero and heroine in the opening scenes, draws the reader into the book to learn what has happened and how three lives will be affected by this unexpected return from the past.

A few pages later, the heroine allows the transient, whom she does not recognize, to move into one of her cottages and do odd jobs in exchange for room and board. This decision sets the plot in motion.

Love Me Forever, Johanna Lindsey's Avon Historical Romance, opens with Lachlan, Laird of Clan MacGregor, coming to the conclusion that being a highwayman does not bring in enough money to fill his coffers. The only solution is to marry a rich woman. The most logical place to find one is in England.

The critical situation in Suzanne Brockman's *Frisco's Kid* (Silhouette Intimate Moments #759) evolves from a serious knee injury Frisco received during a covert operation with the Navy SEALS. In an opening scene, our hero is discharged from the hospital and informed that he is no longer capable of serving in the Navy. It is a crushing blow.

Following the famous advice, "Put your character up a tree and throw rocks at him," the author arranges for Frisco to become the temporary guardian of his sister's five-year-old daughter. For a man who can scarcely look after himself, this is a dreadful burden. These events are observed by Mia, an attractive neighbor, who as a teacher used to working with children, is immediately touch by the child's situation. The author nicely chooses contrasting characters and character flaws that work well to create a hook that's sure to intrigue and conflict that carries the reader through to the end of the book.

If the conflict stems primarily from differences in the characters' personalities or convictions, letting your reader know the hero first can have some advantages. Perhaps one way to decide which protagonist should open the story is to determine whose life is about to undergo the most dramatic change. In this story it is the hero, Frisco, because on the surface it appears his entire world had just fallen apart, leaving him nothing to live for. Contributing to the problem is his alcoholic sister and the history of alcohol in the family background.

I've noticed over a period of several years' membership in writer's critique groups that one of the main problems experienced by both novice and professional writers is a tendency to begin the book in the wrong place. Usually, it is a case of starting too soon. Knowing we must introduce our protagonists and establish them as believable characters, we overwhelm the reader with pages of background information in the first chapter.

This is too frequently achieved via an in-transit scene where the heroine is arriving in a car/airplane/ship and has time alone to think about why she is there and what is about to happen. Sometimes it is the first day on the new job; other times she is going to meet a client or coming home after a long absence.

A better way is to begin the plot with the *critical situation*—the protagonist actively confronting the issue. Then filter in the background information through dialogue, if possible. Of course we want to get to know and care about the heroine, but we can accomplish this in part by seeing how she reacts to the problem with which she must come to terms.

Remember that it is critical in the opening to show how decisions made this day are going to affect them for the rest of their lives.

2. Setup Scenes

Feeding in the primary background information is called a *setup scene*. In other words, you are setting up the characters in order to motivate them for the action that is sure to follow, and for the critical situation which may have already been introduced.

Characters without motivation are like stick figures: wooden, inflexible and unreal. Properly motivated characters not only enrich the plot but are the glue that holds it together.

It is the family and social background of a character that contribute the highest degree of motivation. What happened in your character's past that made her who she is today? As a child, was she unjustly accused of shoplifting? It could explain her vendetta against a chain of department stores. Or maybe your character really was a shoplifter when she was a child. Was someone else (her father?) blamed for the crime? The guilt that the child carries could trigger many different kinds of behavior which would form the basis of a gripping novel.

Before you decide to use a plot such as this, be sure that the line you are writing for will accept such a complex ploy. Your story should begin after the heroine is old enough to fulfill romance novel requirements.

Again referring to *Frisco's Kid*, the author delays the first actual meeting between Frisco and Mia until the second chapter, where she goes into Mia's viewpoint. Assuming that this retired war hero is vintage World War II, Mia decides to invite him to speak to her history class. The initial meeting is cool thanks to Frisco's bitterness at what life has dealt him. They converse until Mia makes disparaging remarks about military men. After that, the battle of wits becomes personal, and most intriguing.

3. Verifying Scenes

These are "must" scenes that you are required to create because you have set up a situation in advance. If your hero or heroine is a geologist or a stockbroker or a bakery store owner, we must see him or her at work at some point in the story. In short: show, don't tell. It is not satisfying to be told our heroine is a wild-animal veterinarian. We want to see her splinting the bird's wing, feeding the raccoon with a baby bottle or cuddling the newborn fawn. These scenes are most powerful when sprinkled throughout the book but should not be used just for effect. As with any scene, they should have a solid reason for being used at that particular place in the plot line.

4. Conflict Scenes

By now we have our major character or characters clearly defined and we know what is at stake for the main protagonists—that is, their goals and the critical situation. To proceed from this point, we must generate conflict.

Conflict between characters is the simultaneous functioning of mutually exclusive ideas or desires. To a lesser degree, conflict might also be considered a contest. But for the purpose of drama, greater impact can be achieved through stronger emotions.

When Jayne Ann Krentz was asked how she avoided making conflict sound contrived, she said, "All fictional conflict is contrived by definition. The trick is to make it look natural, to make it flow gracefully out of the fundamental nature of the two characters. Keep in mind that the conflict will not appear 'invented' if it fits with the personalities of your hero and heroine. When in doubt, ask yourself: Would this character really act this way or am I twisting his or her actions in order to force the plot in a certain direction? If the action feels natural and suits your characters, your conflict will not appear contrived to an editor or to a reader. That's why the most important thing to do in a romance is to establish clearly the personalities of your characters. Then simply make certain they are true to themselves."

The element of conflict is one of the strongest tools a writer has for creating emotion and drama. Within the context of your novel, conflict can work on the psychological as well as physical level. Conflict is a struggle between opposing forces.

The strongest conflict arises from the wants and needs of the characters; it is called *internal conflict*. *External conflict* comes from outside the characters and is best used in combination with internal conflict.

5. Hindrance and Furtherance Scenes

In moving the characters onward toward a goal or the resolution of the conflict, the author must take care not to make the plot too simple. If the goal or resolution is easily achieved, we immediately lose emotional impact, suspense, drama, adventure—whatever it is we are trying to establish within the confines of the plot.

The plot line should be made up of hills and valleys instead of a straight line running from beginning to middle to end. This is true even for mystery and romantic adventure. If we solve the crime too quickly, the work becomes a short story instead of a novel. For this reason, we must create false leads, clues that send our protagonist off in the wrong direction just when she thinks she has the solution.

If the hero and heroine make love too soon in a romance novel, we have lost the opportunity to write that wonderful scene where the reader savors the sweetness of their reconciliation and final commitment. The ringing of a telephone or doorbell has interrupted more than one torrid love scene.

The uniqueness of the hindrance and furtherance scenes in any novel is a remarkably fine measure of the author's creative ability. But remember, although we must progress and regress with forward and backward plot movement, we must never lose the momentum that holds the reader spellbound.

6. The Turn-Around Scene

Hindrance and furtherance scenes are less dramatic than the turn-around scene, which is also a setback to the developing relationship. The turn-around scene is referred to as "the darkest moment" because it seems there is no solution to the problem. It is often preceded by a scene where it appears that everything has come together. All the bridges have been crossed, all the dragons slain, all the misunderstandings explained. And then, fate or some master stroke determines that the greatest dragon of all lies waiting just around the bend. It seems for a time that the obstacles are too great to overcome.

In my Regency historical trilogy, *The Thackery Jewels*, Topaz, the heroine of book three, has fallen in love with Lord Colby, a man who has a strong commitment to preserving the family heritage. He has already declared his love for her when he discovers that she is not truly a Thackery, but an orphan of unknown parentage adopted at birth. This creates a problem that shoots the plot off in a new direction.

In the midlist or single title novel and in the mainstream novel, the turn-around scene is often more subtle, frequently arising out of character growth or fresh insight into a problem. It can be as simple as a wrong decision made, but made for all the right reasons. The solution does not always result in a happy resolution to the problem, as in the romance novel.

The content of the turn-around scene and where it appears depends on the plot, but it most frequently is set in the final third of the book.

Whatever kind of novel you are writing, the turn-around scene is a mandatory, emotion-packed scene and a pivotal point in the book.

Following the turn-around scene, you will have additional scenes to provide hindrance and furtherance. This tension builds until the final resolution at the end.

7. Flashback/Flash Forward Scenes

At some point in the novel, you may possibly want to use the flashback as a device to fit certain information into the novel. It is a ploy in which time stands still while the protagonist thinks back to events that happened previous to the story's opening.

Adequate transitions are a must in order to leave no question in the reader's mind as to what is taking place and in what time period.

Flashback is all too frequently overused. Use it only when the action taking place in the past is stronger, more dramatic than the action taking place in the present. If the flashback is too long, the writer must seriously consider whether or not the book begins in the wrong place.

Flash forwards are even more tricky because they tend to date a book. There was a time when authors used to insert themselves into the narration by writing a passage like: "Ah, but if Carolyn only knew what she was getting into, she would never have accepted the key in the first place."

Another example is where the author writes a passage like: "Ten years from then she would have forgotten all about it, but on that crisp April night, Carolyn took the sailboat out to Jasmine Key and buried the letters under the statue of the bearded lion."

Whenever we have author intrusion it interrupts the flow of reader involvement in the narrative and reminds her that this is, after all, just a story.

8. The Climax Scene

All previously outlined scenes lead the reader to the climax of the novel where the conflict is resolved, and the goal is reached (or if not, a reason is given why the outcome is acceptable). With the romance's focus on relationships, the climax almost always means a firm commitment between the hero and heroine. It is a dramatic point in the book where they recognize and verbalize the fact that, despite their differences, they belong together. It usually involves a love scene, though not necessarily the hottest love scene of the book.

At the climax of the romance novel, the author needs to show that what was at first a significant physical attraction between hero and heroine has now matured into a deeper, more enduring love—a love that rises above personal conflicts.

If the romance novel involves suspense or intrigue, the climax may be the dramatic end of a chase or the solution to the mystery or the containment of the virus strain.

In *The Thackery Jewels*, Topaz is forced to accept Arthur's offer for marriage when Colby turns away. Too late, Colby changes his mind and wants to marry her. This is followed by a series of adventures in which the couple tries to find out who her parents were.

Then, in a stunning discovery, Arthur's mother also learns that Topaz was a misbegotten baby and withdraws her son's marriage proposal. Learning about this scandal, Lady Breckenridge, a wealthy noblewoman, steps forward to claim Topaz as her own daughter. Arthur's mother tries to make amends, but Topaz is relieved to be rid of Arthur, having already fallen in love with Colby. She and Colby assume that Lady Breckenridge has, out of kindness and affection for Topaz, lied to protect her good name.

9. The Conclusion Scene

It is unwise to leave your reader perched on a highly dramatic level. It is best to add a few lines or even a few pages to give your reader an easy letdown. This is the point where you tie up all the loose ends, where you explain all the clues planted in earlier chapters, the point where the reader is contented with a satisfying ending.

In the conclusion of *The Thackery Jewels*, Lady Breckenridge reveals how as a young girl she was forced into marriage to save her beloved family's home. Her future husband would not have accepted her if he had known she had just conceived another man's child. The other man was Quentin Thackery; he eventually adopted his own child.

The conclusion of the book also ties up a subplot involving the impending betrothal of Aunt Prudence, a woman who wore widowhood like a trophy.

The nine types of scenes listed should appear in every romance novel. They contribute significant plot points. Be certain they appear in the right place for proper pacing.

The Opening Chapters

Is there any feeling equal to that special euphoria of beginning to write the first chapter of a new book? The story is all there in your head. You are hooked. The ability to grant the reader that same heady feeling of excitement as she picks up the book and turns to chapter one is the goal toward which every writer strives.

Take the time to study shoppers in a bookstore. Almost without exception, they first select a book by the cover and then turn to the blurb on the back. After that, they open it to page one and read the first few paragraphs; on rare occasions they will turn to the end and read the last few paragraphs. Then, they either decide to buy the book or replace it on the shelf.

Is it any wonder that editors stress the importance of a powerful opening scene?

In the section on dialogue, we discussed the dialogue opening preferred by some editors. It can be a powerful hook, but not all books are suited to a dialogue opening. There are other, equally strong openings.

In Nora Roberts's book *Holding the Dream* (Jove), the opening begins with the heroine's introspection. Kate Powell, the heroine, was still struggling to accept the fact that her family was dysfunctional. Her father was a thief. If she couldn't understand it, she must learn to accept it and get on with her life. She did so by setting strict rules for herself, no shortcuts permitted, because success could only be achieved through her own hard work and dedication to her own strict values. Now an accountant, Kate is strongly motivated to be honest and careful in every aspect of her life. It sets up the compelling story of intrigue, discovery and romance.

There are three schools of thought on how openings should be handled. Some writers and editors believe that the action must come first before the characters are fully drawn. Others are convinced that we must get to know our characters before we involve them in an emotional scene. Still others believe that setting the stage to give the reader a sense of time and place is the crucial element for book beginnings.

At one time, prologues were unsalable. Now you will find many books opening with a prologue. Occasionally a prologue is used as a device to introduce the hero when, without it, the book would go on too long before he makes an appearance. In historical novels, a prologue may set up the political situation of the setting or other aspects of the back story. If a prologue is very long, one must question whether it should be the first chapter. Following the prologue, begin another chapter or space down four lines in the manuscript to indicate when the actual story opens with a critical situation—that is, today's problem. For the novice writer it still is advisable to avoid using a prologue whenever possible.

There is no single correct way to begin all novels. Again, we must return to market analysis and the kind of book we want to write in order to determine the most salable opening for a particular novel.

My own experiences with series romance editors suggest that the most marketable openings are those that create strong reader identification with a sympathetic character, and those in which the story immediately triggers questions in the reader's mind. This doesn't mean we need to know within the first few pages where the heroine was born, whether her parents are still alive, how many men she has been attracted to or even how long she has known the hero. However, it does mean that we must know how she feels at the moment and what critical changes have just taken place or are about to take place in her life. When we are able to understand how a person feels and why she feels what she does, we immediately begin to sympathize with her.

To quote one editor: "Why should I give a damn about how she's going to save the ranch if I don't even give a damn about her?" Good question. It's one we should think about when writing a first chapter.

A character's psychological profile is not to be confused with physical appearance. It is far more important to know what goes on in a character's head than to know what color her eyes are or what she is wearing. It's the difference between knowing a character and knowing about her. Physical descriptions can be fed in later through the hero's dialogue or introspection. The same rule applies to the hero when the book opens in his viewpoint.

How the hero and heroine meet for the first time has always been a problem for romance writers who want to create something different. Again, reading within the genre in order to find out what has already been done is necessary. One editor said at a writer's conference, "If I read one more manuscript where the hero and heroine bump into each other in the corridor and she drops her papers, I'm going to vomit." You can guess what would happen to your manuscript if it contained such a scene. Editors work very hard. They read manuscripts most of the day and more often than not take them home to read at night. Give editors and yourself a break. Avoid clichés.

If you allow events to happen naturally, your reader will believe. Take any arena of action where people come together out of mutual interest or need. Provide the characters with that need, and you have a logical way for them to meet. In a romance novel there should be some sexual recognition in the initial meeting that sets the stage for the real electricity to follow.

Another aspect to be considered in first chapters is the mood or tone of a book, sometimes called the *voice*. Some romance novels rely heavily on mood to carry the story. In such cases it is imperative to establish the mood beginning with the opening lines. Here is an example of the opening lines from Anne Stuart's book *Lord of Danger* (Zebra Historical Novel).

> There were monsters who walked the land. Alys had never seen one in the flesh, but she had no doubt they existed. The nuns who'd raised her and her half-sister Claire were full of warnings, and whether the death-delivering creature was named Beelzebub, Grendel, or Satan, they were all terrifying to a young and believing soul like Alys of Summersedge.
>
> Unlike Claire, Alys was obedient. Fierce when it came to protecting those she loved, but a devout coward when it came to her own welfare. She hated ghost stories and nightmares, thunderstorms and restive horses. She hated birch rods and slaps and angry words, but she would endure them all to protect her sister. She would endure anything.
>
> Even marriage to a bone-cracking, blood-sucking monster.

Notice how the author uses buzzwords to create an underlying sense of impending doom; words like *monsters, warnings, terrifying, Satan, fierce, nightmares, thunderstorms, restive, blood-sucking, bonecracking*. All these words are woven together to create an undercurrent of apprehension and fear.

We immediately sympathize with Alys, who was taken from the protection of a convent to enter into a forced marriage with a man who was best known for his cruelty. We also admire Alys for her determination, despite her fears, to see that no harm came to her sister.

Stella Cameron's historical romance *Dear Stranger*, from Warner Books, opens with an innocent sounding dialogue involving men's body parts. The heroine, best described as unrelenting, is determined to find out what makes men tick, and what they have that drives them to pursue women—a bewitching opening!

As the book continues, we discover how she beseeches the hero to demonstrate just exactly how those body parts work. It is the heroine's innocent curiosity and the hero's frustration that keep those pages turning. The plot of the story unfolds little by little around characters who vibrate with life.

In the most memorable romance novels, first chapters seem to unfold in a formulaic sequence of events: problem, tension, decision, action, consequence. When the hero enters the picture with his opposing attitudes, conflict is interwoven among the five elements and the drama is set in motion.

Each chapter should lead naturally into the next chapter to give the plot momentum and continuity. This is more important in the romance novel than in single title novels, which may have an abrupt change of time, place, characters or viewpoint.

10

Sensuality vs. Sexuality

One question beginning romance writers always ask is "How much sex do you have to put in the book?" The question requires a careful answer. For one thing, if a writer feels that you *have* to put sex in a book, it would seem to indicate that writing a sensual scene makes the writer uncomfortable. If it does, then it also seems logical that the scene would not ring true, and then the reader would also feel uncomfortable.

It is important to write the kind of book you like to read. Both Harlequin Romance and Silhouette Romance lines are "sweet" romances; the characters do not go to bed together until they are safely married. The same holds true for inspirational and Christian romances.

The saying "Sex sells" is certainly true. Sit in on several author book signings and you'll soon discover that most readers first pick up the books with sexy covers. But there is a growing market for inspiration; if this is your preference, go for it.

Think about it. What is romance? The dictionary definition is less than satisfactory. Anyone who has experienced falling in love knows that it takes more than a "strong, usually short-lived attachment" to constitute romance.

In the same way, it takes more than putting your characters into bed to make a romance novel. The problem lies in the confusion between the words *sexual* and *sensual*. It is the sensuality, the tension of impending sexual fulfillment that makes romance novels exciting. Before that can begin to happen, the writer must create vibrations: the incredible first moment when one (or both) of the protagonists recognizes the intense pull of sexual attraction toward a particular person.

In Dorothy Garlock's *Larkspur* (Warner Books Historical Novel ©1997) Kristin, an Easterner, has inherited a Montana ranch only to learn that land grabbers will do anything to prevent her from taking it over. Her only hope is to trust in Buck Lenning, the hard-bitten hired man. Lenning knows he must protect her, but it is all he can do to keep watch over his senile father who cannot be left alone. The solution: ask this handsome "old maid" to move in with him until the will can be finalized.

> A tightness crept into his throat, and he thought how foolish he was to think that she'd even consider such a thing. She would be sure that he was an ignorant, ill-mannered, saddle tramp hoping to get her share of the Larkspur.
>
> She was looking him over with the same degree of interest as he was looking at her. The straightforwardness of her stare convinced him that there was nothing pretentious about her and that her expression of compassion for Moss was real.

A few paragraphs later, he suggests she move in as his housekeeper. When she agrees to look after his house and his father in exchange for Lenning's protection:

> Buck grasped her slender hand tightly in his large rough one. When she smiled, her eyes moved over him like a touch. Watching her lips spread and her eyes light up, he was filled with a quiet peace. He suddenly felt the desire to hold this soft woman in his arms, kiss her lips and beg her to stay here in this house he had painstakingly built and tried to furnish, and to care for him in all the ways a woman cared for her man.
>
> The thought was so real that before he could comprehend what was happening, his own body responded to his thoughts. He dropped her hand quickly and turned to Moss, who had risen from his chair.

The secret to creating compelling scenes of sensuality is to feed in the impressions slowly and let the need grow with each passing encounter.

It must not be overlooked that the degree of sexuality in romance novels differs greatly from publisher to publisher and line to line. While descriptions such as "His fingers dug into her flesh," and "His mouth hurt as it took her lips by force; the insistent pressure bruised and hurt . . ." were once perfectly acceptable in some lines, they are unlikely to survive in most of today's markets. Requirements change frequently and the best way to keep up-to-date, short of having an editor as a best friend, is to study recent guidelines and read recently published books. Famous-name authors are able to stretch the boundaries of guidelines a bit more than unknown authors. Take this fact into consideration when analyzing the markets. When you buy a romance novel for research, be very sure to check the date of publication. Some publishers bring out old novels under new names.

When romance novels first became popular, it was understood that there would be no action below the belt until the heroine was legally married. Even then the actual sex act was simply alluded to. Then, as older heroines were introduced, the hero was allowed a few more liberties before marriage, but the moment the clothes started to come off, the reader was gently but firmly ushered out the bedroom door. At the same time, there was no doubt in the reader's mind that as soon as the sun peeked over the horizon, the couple would rush out to apply for their marriage license.

When more realistic (or if you prefer, modern) heroines became popular, the foreplay scenes became so overheated that the reader was able to open the bedroom door just far enough to see a little of what was going on inside, but the bed covers remained in place.

My editor at Jove finally said, "Look, you're driving me nuts. You can't take us this far and not put them in bed." And so I wrote my first completed love scene.

Around 1980 more barriers disappeared. One romance line required that there must be one bed scene by the third chapter and at least three bed scenes in the whole book. I use the term "bed scene" lightly, because competition among writers was intense to see who could invent the most exotic (and uncomfortable) place for lovers to get together. There were closet scenes, anthill scenes, love among the pine needles and lovemaking under water. One very memorable scene took place in the bathroom.

The pendulum swings. Wiser heads prevailed, and editors decreed that fantasy had reached beyond the romantic to the ridiculous. New guidelines were drawn up saying it was illogical for the characters to hop into bed an hour or two after they met.

Romance novels should reflect a developing relationship, with the characters first having an opportunity to get to know each other intellectually before they get to know each other in the biblical sense.

And so the characters cooled it for a while. Once they decided the time was right, they made love with an energy and passion that was superhuman.

The current trend is to build the story layer-by-layer, allowing the ultimate sex scene to be the fulfillment of careful preparation on the part of the writer. But again, do your homework. Each line has its own imprint.

One rule remained constant for several years. Very few romance lines would accept clinical names for below-the-belt male and female sex organs. One author quipped, "I'd give half of my next royalty check to come up with a good name for 'his male hardness.' " An accepted and practical description now being used by a few publishers is "an erection," but some publishers now accept clinical descriptions.

That writer echoed the sentiments of other writers who have searched in vain for a substitute for the Victorian euphemism for a female's "gates of paradise." Whatever you do, avoid flowery descriptions of vital parts. Although humor is possible in a love scene, we want the reader to laugh *with* us, not *at* us.

Sex in the romance novel has come a long way, but as sure as there are birds and bees, the pendulum will swing again. In the late 1980s, with the reality of the AIDS epidemic sweeping across the world, some writers chose to recognize what they called "a responsibility to our readers" and introduced protected sex to their novels.

There are three schools of thought on how sexual protection should be handled in the romance novel: (1) By spelling out how the hero (or heroine) excused himself and went to the dresser to get a condom. (2) By merely alluding to the fact that they took care to protect the other person. For example: She said, "Wait. I have something in the drawer. I'm sure you'll feel better knowing that we are both safe." (3) Avoiding the subject and letting the reader logically assume that such intelligent, caring people would never risk their own life or that of their lover.

Sexual protection is not something new to romance novels. In the early 1980s one or two short-lived romance lines experimented with explicit sexual protection for birth control. While a few liberated readers applauded the message, most readers felt that it detracted from the fantasy. Whether the message was too boldly stated or whether other elements contributed to its demise, the technique of teaching the reader about birth control never became popular.

Time will answer the question of whether the writer should speak out for safe sex or leave it for the reader to assume the characters are not stupid. But whichever way you choose, when writing series romance, write it with a light hand. No one likes to be hit over the head with advice.

Senior Editor Leslie Wainger of Silhouette Books says, "Regarding safe sex, a hotly discussed subject these days, I think several points need to be made. The first is that none of us must ever forget why these books are so popular. They owe their success entirely to the fact that they provide an escape from real life. Though they must be very much a part of the world we live in and reflect the changing role of women and the changing face of women's dreams, they must not be an exact reflection of that world or they will cease to fulfill the reader's needs. Therefore, too much realism—on any score—destroys the fantasy we are providing, and that includes the discussion of safe sex. Birth control, treated in a way that doesn't tear the fabric of fantasy, has been a part of these books for a long time, and the hero's offer to 'protect' the heroine can certainly be taken in many ways. If the current real-life uneasiness over sexual mores does have an effect in the books, it's more likely to be in general terms: characters with less of a 'past,' less of an expectation for early lovemaking, or lovemaking based on less of a commitment—in the more sensuous lines—and so on. Realistic concerns are definitely a part of these books, but in ways that still allow the fantasy of the perfect romance to remain paramount."

I was fascinated by a poll taken among readers of a popular women's magazine. It asked, "What was your most romantic moment?" The answers were surprising. Some of them were: "When he sent me a single red rose to say he was sorry." "The night that he brought me a hot fudge sundae." "When he held my hand and talked to me during labor pains." "The little love notes he puts under my pillow before he goes out of town."

Almost none of the romantic moments had anything to do with the physical aspect of lovemaking beyond kissing and hugging. Of course we have to take into consideration that it was a poll of women. It might be interesting to find how a poll of men would answer the same question. Nevertheless, romance novels are read primarily by women.

100

When analyzing the sex in a romance novel, we should first remember that sex is not the prime requirement for a romance. It is through sensuality that our bodies prepare us for the ultimate sex act: by veiled looks across a crowded room; the first time he touches your hand; the first time you are alone together; the first time he sends you flowers; the first time he tells you how special you are to him; the way his gaze keeps coming back to you; and his way of touching you casually, yet with a secret intimacy that you feel deep in the marrow of your bones. One by one, this feast of the senses builds until the mere mention of his name floods your body with warmth.

And then there are the accoutrements of sensuality: the napkin with the imprint of her lips; her sweater that still holds her own special scent; tickets torn in half from last night's ballet; letters in his dear, scrawling handwriting; words to your favorite song; the imprint of his head on the pillow; a snapshot torn in half; a phone call in the middle of the night to tell you how much he needs you.

Sensual impressions that create sexual tension are the things romance is made of. Just as characterization consists of layers of experience, romance is born out of everyday things that trigger the emotional responses to a special someone. And then, inevitably, the body cries out for fulfillment and the moment arrives when two individuals recognize a mutual need to unite as a single entity.

A beginning writer might describe the culmination of the sex act as waves crashing against the shore, fireworks that light up the night sky, or with any number of awe-inspiring clichés. It takes genuine creativity to find a new and compelling way to describe a climax. It also takes imagination to create foreplay that is sensual but does not culminate immediately in the sex act. Remember, anticipation is key.

Here is another scene from *Dear Stranger* by Stella Cameron (Warner Books).

> They kissed.
> He'd told her it would be wrong, but that he wanted to kiss her and do a great deal more. And she had said, "So would I."
> Amazing girl.
> Wait. Don't rush this. Give her time. But her lips opened a little so that he felt the moistness within. A rush of heat overtook him, heat and tension in his skin, and beneath his skin. Brushing, brushing, he tilted his lips over hers, back and forth, urging the

way a little wider but not daring to go too far.

Her fingertips were like moths at his jaw, then beneath the open neck of his shirt. Eager, seeking fingers that explored—and drove him wild. . . .

(Then a line or two later . . .)

Her tongue slipped along his bottom lip.

No man who held her, looked into her dove eyes, would do other than send up prayers of gratitude.

She drank him in without knowing she drained him.

His shirt parted company with his shoulders, pushed aside so that this quiet miss could expand her knowledge.

This is just a mild beginning to a charming, very funny and sensual love story. One is not even put off when in her innocence, the heroine defines man's mysterious part as his "Supreme Scepter." You have to read this one.

The first few minutes that *follow* a love scene should not be overlooked because the sensitivity between the hero and the heroine are an indication to the reader that the lovemaking was not intended to be a one-night stand, but a fulfillment.

Notice that the scene was written completely from the hero's viewpoint. It is unlikely that this technique would have been used a few years ago. Fortunately for both writer and reader, some editors are willing to take a chance. Cameron has succeeded in creating a hero who is strong yet caring and sensitive.

In the category romance, it must be remembered that once the heroine meets the hero, there must be no other man for her. It is unlikely that she is a virgin, as the heroine was in the early romances, though it is possible if she is properly motivated. But to make the heroine sympathetic to our readers, she cannot have been promiscuous.

In addition, our heroine should not use sex as a weapon. No doubt there is some book out there where this ploy was part of an excellent plot, but for the beginning writer, it is safer to use a different approach.

In the single title romance or midlist novel, as well as the mainstream novel, this limitation does not exist. There is usually less emphasis on one man, one woman, than some overriding problem that threatens to destroy lives.

Editor Debra Matteucci says, "Readers like to see the protagonists getting acquainted and overcoming conflicts—both personal and interpersonal—and falling in love. Instead of the antagonism that is so often prevalent in these scenarios, I prefer to see a gradual learning process, an exploration of each other's personality and ethics."

Booksellers say their customers complain about a lack of warmth in today's romances. "Warmth doesn't mean hot love scenes all the time," Matteucci explains. "Sometimes the characters don't seem to care about what they're doing. There's too much emphasis on sex and not enough on the relationship." What readers want for their heroine is cuddling and hugging, and the warmth of commitment. Hot sex scenes are all right only if the book calls for them, but too often they are added to books just for effect.

Interestingly enough, romance novels sold to foreign markets are sometimes edited to soften the physical side of lovemaking. This is true both in France and Italy where readers seem to prefer sensuality as opposed to overt sexuality.

There will come a time in your career as a romantic writer when someone (usually a reporter or interviewer out to create excitement) will say something like, "How can you write such trash? It's nothing but pornography."

Your response might be: "Do you consider love between man and woman pornography? Pornography is sex used out of greed to satisfy one's own needs without thought about pleasing your partner. It has nothing to do with lovemaking. We write about the magic of falling in love."

These are just a few series romance authors who are admired for their ability to convey strong sexual tension and convey sensual love scenes: Ann Maxwell, Nora Roberts, Jayne Ann Krentz, Dorothy Garlock, Heather Graham, Sandra Brown, Janet Dailey, LaVyrle Spencer, Catherine Coulter, Johanna Lindsey and Anne Stuart.

Exercise

Study recently published novels and make a list of the steps in which authors show the development of sexual tension from the first acknowledgment of attraction to the actual love scene.

Use the headings of the five senses and make your own list of things that can trigger a romantic response: fragrances (not just flowers or perfume, but other scents like melted candle wax or the heady musk of perspiration); the feel of his tweed jacket against your bare arm; satin sheets; a sip of cognac; soft music; the way the hair on his wrist curls around the band of his wristwatch. Be creative.

11

The Historical Romance Novel

Historical novels surged to the forefront of popularity in the 1980s, and although they have changed from their original concept, they continue to command a large portion of shelf space in most bookstores.

It is incorrect to assume that one must have a degree in history to write a historical romance. Nothing could be further from the truth. What is needed is an inquisitive mind, the time and energy to do the required research, and a careful attention to detail. If you hate to read historical novels, you will probably not only dislike the work involved in researching and writing them, but you are likely to cheat the reader by not doing your best work. Many readers say they not only enjoy the romance and excitement of historicals, but they feel they are learning something about the history of a different place and era.

Historical novels are as old as the publishing industry. Some historicals, such as books by James Oliver Curwood, C.S. Forester and Rafael Sabatini, have become literary classics.

More recent authors, such as Margaret Mitchell and her *Gone With the Wind*, and Kathleen Winsor, who wrote *Forever Amber*, have triggered significant changes in the development of historical novels by including scenes of passion.

There is hardly a reader who is not familiar with the names Mary Stewart and Victoria Holt, two authors who brought a Gothic element to the historical novel. It was when Kathleen Woodiwiss sold her novel *The Flame and the Flower* that sex became a focal point in the historical novel and publishers realized that sex sells books.

It was about this time that *bodice-ripper*, an unkind but generally accepted term for books featuring a heavy dose of passion and rape, came into usage. Rosemary Rogers's book *Sweet Savage Love*, with its sexual smorgasbord, hit the stands with a sales record that stood the industry on its head. But times change and so does the public's appetite. Bodice-rippers, with their sex and violence, are now hard to find. Still, they introduced an element of flaming passion that has evolved into the highly sensual historical romance novel of today.

When editors are questioned at writer's conferences about what they are looking for in a historical novel, 100 percent of those I've heard respond said that they would not buy a novel in which the heroine is raped. Yet occasionally one gets through. There are no absolutes in this business.

With the burgeoning market for historicals came a wealth of new writers whose names soon became recognized: LaVyrle Spencer, Rebecca Brandywine, Roberta Gellis, Shirlee Busbee, Bertrice Small, Patricia Matthews, Sylvie Sommerfield and Jennifer Blake, to name just a few. Some of them are still popular and dozens of other names can be added to the list: writers such as Amanda Quick, Anne Stuart, Candice Hern, Stella Cameron, Susan Plunkett, Heather Graham, Kate Kingsley, Cassie Edwards and Johanna Lindsey. The list of successful authors is very extensive, as you will soon discover when cruising the historical romance section in bookstores.

Even as the markets expanded, historical novels divided into categories and subcategories. There are juvenile and young adult historical novels that are usually hardcover and are distributed to libraries. These books are often based on factual incidents with a fictional character in the viewpoint role. Young adult or juvenile historicals nearly always feature a young protagonist. The protagonist can either be a famous person, as in purely historical novels, or a fictional character involved with a historical character or incident.

An excellent source for names of publishers and their current requirements is the most recent edition of *Writer's Market* (new each September from Writer's Digest Books). You'll find addresses, contact names, submission requirements and more.

Author Ethel Herr has created a series called The Seekers, from Bethany House Publishers. *The Dove and the Rose*, first in the series, is set during the political revolts of the sixteenth century when Holland revolted against the forces Spain's King Phillip sent to squelch the rebellion and abolish religious heresy. This book won the Silver Angel Award for excellence in Christian writing.

Among adult historical novels, the most popular or most salable is the single title historical romance offered by most major publishers. They stress a compelling love story between the hero and heroine, embellished with all the accoutrements of historical costumes and setting. The conflict often weaves the details of the historical setting and events with human emotions to create a compelling drama.

The *western romance* is a category of historical novel that deals primarily with the westward movement in America. Among the authors who have made a name in this specialized field are Joyce Brandon and Georgina Gentry. Kathleen Eagle and Janelle Taylor are well known for their novels featuring Native Americans. There is still a hungry market for these stories.

Regency Historicals

The Regency historical has a following of dedicated readers who are enthralled by the period in English history from 1811 to 1820, when the Prince of Wales gained control of the throne during the illness of King George III. It was during that time that Jane Austen wrote *Pride and Prejudice* and her other novels of wit and manners. In our day, Georgette Heyer became the chronicler of those times and her books are considered essential reading for anyone wishing to explore the Regency category.

A few purists resent the latitude allowed today's author in writing the Regency novel, but the new generation of readers is delighted with the somewhat broader view of Regency society. Traditional Regency romances (the markets are dwindling) still maintain the comedy of manners theme, but a degree of sensuality, as well as elements of adventure and intrigue, has been added.

A play on words, snappy repartee, formal language, ruffled feelings, and embarrassing situations all give flavor and humor to the Regency style.

The much longer Regency historical novels include obvious sexuality and subjects such as time travel and wizardry as well as mystery and adventure.

To be able to write with accuracy about this period, you must read voraciously to understand the special language that is the keystone of the Regency novel. The rules for writing the Regency historical novel are restrictive, but the challenge is exciting and rewarding to the prolific writer who may develop a following of loyal fans.

There is a wealth of research material available on this fascinating time. A list of sources may be found in the section on reference materials in the back of this book.

Candice Hern is well known for her well-researched traditional Regency novels. She says: "One of the reasons I enjoy writing Regency romances is the challenge of the social setting: a highly structured Society governed by strict rules of conduct based on gender, marital status, rank and position. Placing characters within the confines of such a rigid social structure provides immediate avenues of conflict, where the protagonists may have to struggle against prescribed restrictions in order to develop a love relationship, or, equally difficult, to play strictly by the rules.

"But those pesky rules can pose problems for the writer. For example, it can be very difficult to infuse sexual tension into a story where the hero and heroine are barely allowed to touch one another with propriety, much less hop into bed. Unless the heroine is a widow (who can get away with more flaunting of the rules) or a wife, sexual intimacy is generally not appropriate in a Regency. Wives and widows have therefore become more and more popular as Regency heroines, allowing the writer to stay within the rules and still explore the sexual aspects of a relationship.

"The tricky part, though, for writers of traditional Regencies is to develop sexual tension with characters who must behave realistically within the limitations imposed by Regency Society. In the most successful Regencies, this is accomplished by pulling the reader right into the characters' heads so that it is clear what they are thinking and feeling, despite what their actions and words may outwardly portray.

"Introspection, reflection and internal monologue therefore become important elements of character development and sexual tension in a Regency. Unfortunately, these are also devices that can bring pacing to a grinding halt. So, what's a writer to do?

"In my own Regencies, I like to use internalization during dialogue to reveal sexual tension. This method is less likely to slow down the pace of the story than, for example, long passages of subsequent reflection. While face to face with the heroine during dialogue, the hero can silently interpret, or simply notice, gestures, body language and eye contact in ways that build sexual tension. Awareness of such details as the curve of an ear, the arch of a brow, the nape of a neck, can go a long way to increase sexual tension in a traditional Regency. Sprinkling dialogue with beats of physical observation pulls the reader further into the character's head, thus enriching overall characterization while at the same time planting seeds of sexual tension.

In the example below from *A Garden Folly* (Signet Regency Romance), the hero pauses for a bit of introspection during a leisurely conversation with the heroine. This passage illustrates the social restrictions placed on the characters' behavior. He cannot do what he wants to do—kiss her—not only because it would break the rules placed on unmarried couples, but also because of his position. He is posing as a gardener, and in that role he is confined by rules of both gender and position.

> She turned back to her painting, and Stephen was almost spellbound by the vision of her in the Old Hall garden, the sun behind her inflaming the soft blond curls peeking out from beneath her bonnet. He had an absurd desire to reach out and touch one of those curls. Would it feel as silky as it looked? What he really wanted to do was remove that jaunty little chip straw bonnet and see her hair in all its glory, unpinned and spilling in golden waves down her back. But perhaps her hair was not even long, as he liked to imagine, but was cropped fashionably short. The fact that he did not know made him realize he had never seen her without a hat. What would she do if he asked her to remove it?
>
> What would she do if he reached down and kissed her? But he could not do that. He knew he could not. But that was all right, for it was pleasure enough just to look at her. For now, it was enough.

Candice Hern uses narrative to set the backdrop but she uses the viewpoint character as a vehicle to inform the reader, thus keeping the reader in the scene. Here is an excerpt from *An Affair of Honor* (Signet Regency Romance).

> Meg held an anxious Bristol Blue in place on a slight rise near the southern boundary of Thornhill's land. The unusual land ridge, thought to be the remnants of an ancient barrow, overlooked the road as it wound its way through the wide, flat clay loams on its way to join the Ixworth Road. Just below Meg's position, the road came to a small stone bridge spanning a narrow portion of the

Black Bourne. Screened from view by a well-timbered hedgerow and a stand of elm trees, she had a clear prospect of the river and the road. A jackdaw screeched as its gray head swooped down toward the fat clumps of marsh marigolds edging the river, and Bristol danced and nickered in his impatience to be off. Meg stroked his neck to calm him as she watched the black-and-yellow carriage make its way across the stone bridge.

"Good bye, Sedge," she whispered.

A single tear rolled down her cheek as the carriage disappeared from view into the thick woodlands beyond.

Mainstream Historicals

Some mainstream historical novels have an element of romance but are steeped more strongly in actual history. Often they are plotted around fact but contain many elements of fiction. The term *faction* has been coined for this kind of novel because it is fictionalized fact. The stories use real individuals from history for the viewpoint instead of using real characters as secondary or functional characters who merely set the stage. The dialogue and some of the scenes are created out of the writer's imagination, but they must ring true to what the real characters might have said and done. It is important not to restructure history. Know your real characters well, so you don't have them attending a gathering in Paris when they were actually in Bombay at the time.

The *roman-fleuve*, commonly called the saga or generational novel, is another form of historical novel. The plotline deals primarily with families caught up in the conflict of the times and usually spans three or more generations. The term, coined by Romain Rolland, is derived from the fact that the development of the plot is "now swift, now slow" like the flow of a river.

A common technique used in writing the saga is to have one character, such as a powerful or domineering matriarch or patriarch of the family, who survives throughout the three generations (or at least the person's influence survives) and is the red thread that gives the story cohesion. It may also be a family business that ties the stories together.

These action-filled novels are packed with the drama of families torn apart by greed, war, jealousy, misunderstandings and revenge— all the bigger-than-life emotions that create enough drama and conflict to hold the reader through the 150,000 or more words that make up these big, mainstream books.

It always creates a strong plot point to surprise the reader and kill off a character or two who seemed to be a vital part of the book. But I was reminded by a speaker at a writer's conference to never kill off too many characters in a novel because it all but eliminates the possibility of a sequel, should your admiring fan club demand one. Good advice!

The *Gothic historical* is a mood piece set in historical times. The market for these is minimal compared to the market for romantic historicals, but a well-crafted historical Gothic has a possibility of selling. Gothics are often less sensual than historical romances because the emphasis is centered on the implied or real threat to the life of our heroine or someone to whom she is close. The setting is usually remote and isolated, so our heroine is left in the most vulnerable position possible.

Frequently the lines are blurred between the various categories of historical novels. They may include time travel, or mystery and adventure as well as a rollicking good love story. This is where an author can experiment to create a unique and compelling plot.

Time Travel

Susan Plunkett, author of a time travel romance for Jove's Historical Time Passages line, says:

"The time travel element poses many challenges to the hero and heroine—and the writer. All three come together from very different cultures, face obstacles, solve problems and believe in love and each other enough for a happy ending. How does a writer achieve this? When writing a time travel romance, keep the following in mind:

- First and foremost, the story is the romance. Time travel is an element of the story. Don't get sidetracked.
- Keep the time travel element simple.
- Avoid the use of time machines. H.G. Wells already did this.
- Avoid getting too technical. Use your imagination to conjure an innovative method of moving through time.
- Avoid becoming immersed in a time paradox. For example, would a man who traveled through time and killed his great-grandfather ever be born?
- Leave the historical facts of the time unaltered. Events surrounding historical milestones are fair game for literary license. History is history.

■ When plotting your story, have the hero or heroine go through time early. Putting the hero and heroine together right away moves the story forward.

■ Keep your characters true to their own time. This is particularly important at the beginning of the story. Words have different meanings through time. Vocabulary miscues can be a marvelous vehicle for humor, misunderstanding, drama, miscommunication and character building through dialogue.

What Does the Time Traveler Face?

Susan Plunkett continues, "The time traveler does not have the luxury of denying the change in time. The character must have an ability to accept, if not understand, the leap through time. If the character stays confused for too long, the story bogs down. He or she must go about solving immediate problems, falling in love, achieving goals and dealing with the changes. The traveler encounters strange customs regardless of the direction he or she moved. The character moving back in time loses modern conveniences formerly taken for granted. However, this character brings a different perspective of history, culture and society.

"Imagine your character with the flu. No tissues or over-the-counter medicines. Cooking on a hearth instead of a microwave or modern stove. Candles instead of light bulbs. No central heat in a Minnesota winter.

"Taken together, these seem overwhelming. In an effort to enlighten the reader, the writer may feel compelled to go into detailed account of the time-shift ramifications. Resist.

"Show the conflict through action and dialogue. By doing so, the story's depth increases, the characters reveal themselves to one another (and the reader) and the plot advances.

"Before you begin outlining your next time travel novel, answer the following questions.

1. Can the story take place without time travel? If so, it probably is not a time travel story. Write the story as a contemporary or historical, as befits it. Using the time travel element as a gimmick because you think it will help sell the story usually comes across as just that.

2. Does the time travel element profoundly impact the romance between the heroine and hero? If so, this is a valid time travel story.

3. Are the complexities and influences of time travel woven through-out the story? Are they critical in terms of external and/or internal character conflict? If you cannot answer an emphatic "Yes," rethink your story. Time travel must be an integral part of the character goals, motivation and conflict.

"Time travel isn't something that happens in the first couple of chapters, then fades into the background. It impacts everything: outlook; background; mores; culture; expectations; language; yes, even religion and politics in some cases. The greatest common denominator the heroine and hero have is each other. Therein lies the story."

Among Susan Plunkett's time travel books is *Heaven's Time* (Jove Time Passages). Susan's heroine is an astronaut who is transported back in time after a space accident.

When the heroine eventually regains consciousness, she is deep in the middle of a lake, completely nude. And so begins her new life in a new time. Fascinating.

Here is another example of how the time transportation might be done. This is the beginning of chapter one.

The dome was creepy this time of night. The floodlights were shut down after midnight to give the plants time to rest. Except for the standard utility lamp, only a shaft of moonlight streaking through the many-paned glass enclosure illuminated the place where she waited. Ann Windsor was angry. Angry at everyone concerned with the project, but especially angry with Jacob Speare. Nothing new there. Their once-budding romance came to a shrieking halt the day he betrayed her.

She paced inside the small circle of light. "Of all people, Jake, why did the director have to choose you to be the observer?"

"I volunteered."

"I'll just bet you did. It's so silly anyway. I don't need company. I've worked past midnight many times and been perfectly safe. That's why they need a night watchman."

"You're losing your perspective, Ann. By all calculations the Helix Bulbophyllum isn't scheduled to bloom for over a week. You have no business keeping watch until Wednesday at the earliest." He must have remembered their last argument because he raised his palms outward. "Okay, okay, I didn't mean to be judgmental."

"That's once. Anyway, you're wrong Jake. I have this gut feeling that . . ." She strode to the table where the intensity of the light shone directly on the bulging helix. "Look, can't you see the way she has changed in the last two days? She's ready, Jake, I know it. This is a once in a lifetime experience. No one in recent history has ever seen the helix at the moment it bursts into bloom. The legend says . . ."

"I know what it says. 'When the helix blooms the beauty is such that heavens open and time stands still.' " He reached over and flicked a spiny leaf with his forefinger. A bit of silver fuzz clung to his nail. He flipped it off. "That's what I think of legends."

"Don't do that! I don't want her touched."

"Oh for God's sake, Ann. You speak of it as if it were human."

"To me she is, as well as being my claim to fame. Move over, I want to make sure the spotlight is working for the camera set-up." She cued up light and checked the focus for the tenth time. "It looks good. The heat feels great. I didn't realize it was so . . . Wait!" She froze, her hand poised in midair. "Did you hear that?"

"What?"

"That crackle. Like someone stepping on peanut shells." A tremor of anticipation ran down the backs of her legs. "Something's happening."

He moved closer. "I don't see anything. It's your imagination."

He had no more said the words when the spiral began to shake. A sound like the soft whisper of wind at a high elevation emerged from the base of the stem. At the same moment the swelling rose upward, smoothly negotiating each curve of the helix.

"Camera, Camera," Jake shouted.

"It's on. Oh my God," Ann cried, fighting back the tears. "It's going to bloom. I knew it. Look!"

They leaned close. As they watched a silvery-blue sheen of moisture covered the helix. The bulbous swelling, pale gold in color, grew larger as it reached the top of the spiral and began to settle into place. The gold color darkened to a soft brown as the flower hardened and the opening petals made a crackling sound like crinkled cellophane. Leaning closer, they saw the anthers unfold and the stigma uncoil between them.

Suddenly it shot out a cloud of rust-colored mist into the air for several feet in each direction.

"Wow. Look at that! Did you ever see . . . ?" Ann gasped.

"Never. I . . ." Jake coughed. "What the h. . . ! Ann?" He grabbed her hand. "Your face . . . it's turned color."

She barely heard him. His face had changed shape, contorting first, then elongating before it returned to normal. Everything around them moved in waves of pulsating energy. There was a keening sound as the floor of the dome turned on its side and a gust of wind ripped through the palms and banana trees like an unleashed tornado.

She wanted to scream but the sound died in her throat. Jake's hand held hers in a death grip as a vortex of light and sound swirled around them.

"Jake!" It was all she could manage. He pulled her against him as they were drawn up in a tube of light that glowed with iridescent colors like a crystalized rainbow. Then everything went dark and her brain shut down.

Developing the Historical Romance Plot

Conflict, critical situations, characterization and plot in the historical novel are created in much the same way they are in the contemporary novel.

All the elements necessary to the contemporary plot must also appear in the historical novel. However, the setting and the background story are given more attention because a writer must draw the reader into the time and place in order to loosen the ties that bind us to the contemporary world.

Again, let me emphasize the need for accuracy. Many readers become experts on historical fact and trivia. The intrusion of mistakes, such as a heroine sucking on a sugar cube when they had not yet been invented, is enough to destroy the author's credibility. A reader may not write to the publisher to say how much she liked the book, but you can count on a letter if she discovers an error.

Certain time periods are more salable than others. Editors consider a book historical if the plot takes place before the 1900s. The millennium may change this. A book set in the Dark Ages would probably not lend itself to romance; it is difficult to sell a book set during any time when civilization was at an extremely low ebb. Of course the literary historical might be an exception to this rule, but it should be noted that the literary novel is more difficult to write and to sell.

At this point, books set in Egypt, Africa, the Arctic and most of the South American countries do not sell well. But consider the fickle market and study it well. By next month, the market may take an abrupt turn in another direction. There was a time when manuscripts on India could only find a home in the back of the closet. Then came *The Jewel in the Crown*, and a new fad was created.

Ideas Come From Many Sources

You can find ideas for the historical novel by browsing through the reference section of the library, visiting a museum, surfing the Internet or looking into your own family history. Whenever my husband and I travel, we pick up literature in motel lobbies about nearby historic places. We don't always visit them, but sometimes the brochures trigger ideas and I at least have an address with which to work.

One example of this was when Ed and I went to Florida to research a book. I discovered literature about a once-popular religious group who believed that civilization lived in the center of the earth instead of on the surface. They didn't advocate sex between men and women. Can you imagine the intensity of the conflict between two young people who were torn between their religion and their undeniable need for each other?

Author Joan Wendt stresses the importance of choosing a time period that includes some dramatic historical event. Such an event grounds the book in reality and creates the driving action for the plot or a subplot. Joan Wendt tells of her attempt to set her first novel in London in a period when the only important event that took place was the paving of sidewalks at Westminster. Not exactly an earth-shattering event. She adds that it isn't necessary to use the actual event in the context of the book, but drama and conflict result when you show how the event affected the lives of the protagonists.

LaVyrle Spencer says, "Justification is the key to creating acceptable conflict. Take a conflict that would in other books appear contrived, but justify it to the reader and he or she will accept it readily."

Spencer goes on to say that she takes contrived conflict and wraps it in such engrossing characterization that the reader becomes involved. She asks herself if she would believe it if she were reading it for the first time. If the answer is *no*, she takes it out.

Hindrance and furtherance in the historical novel can be achieved through outside problems faced by the protagonists, as well as the problems that evolve through their personal relationships. War, famine, a gold rush, a fire that destroys a town, inability to communicate because the telephone had not yet been invented, strict social codes preventing a couple from getting together, even the fact that women were cosidered inferior to men—any of these things could shape the development of the relationship between the hero and heroine. These problems provide built-in conflict. In other words, drama.

The Value of Time Lines

There are two kinds of time lines with which a writer should become familiar. The first applies to any kind of writing, whether it be fiction or nonfiction. It simply involves keeping a chronological record of the events in your story or article to ensure they appear in the right sequence or within the right time period. It does not mean that events should or must occur in chronological order within the plot line. What it does mean is that knowing when certain events took place will prevent your heroine from carrying her unborn baby for nineteen months, as happened in one book, or letting a ship cross the ocean in the early 1800s in less than two weeks when it normally took a minimum of a month in a freshening wind.

A pad of paper kept next to your computer makes it easy to jot down significant names and dates as they occur, much easier than tracing back through files or pages to refresh your memory. The longer the book, the more vital it is to keep your details on file as you write.

The second kind of time line deals with research. It applies most often to the writer of historical novels but can be used by all writers who wish to tie their plot into a certain time frame. Basically, the time line is a chronological listing of events during a specific period in a specific place. A description and listing of time line books will be found in the chapter on research.

It isn't easy at first to switch from the contemporary period to the historical period and back again, but the results are worth the challenge. One way to achieve the proper mindset is to restrict your reading to material of a selected time period when you are about to make the change. It will help tune your ear to the proper voice or tone required in that kind of novel.

While exploring the various historical categories, you will soon discover there are other markets available to you if you keep an open mind. Television dramas feature at least one historical per year. Your research can pay off through articles written for regional and historical periodicals. Historical societies often sponsor contests featuring articles written about a certain area or time. Check *Writer's Market* for outlets for both fiction and nonfiction historical material.

12

Writing for the Young Adult and Inspirational Markets

*I*n the early 1980s, the young adult (YA) paperback trend was the hottest new thing in the romance market. Kids turned on to soaps, then discovered series novels aimed at the problems and pleasures of being a teen. Many of the lines popular at that time have disappeared, but there are still a number of publishers who supply the YA market.

Trends affect the YA market in the same way they affect the adult market. Where once the main focus of the YA novel was simply the first awakenings of boy-girl relationships, the market evolved to the heavier problems with which young people had to deal. Now the markets have broadened into a more honest treatment of the teen scene, as well as the Christian market and the purely entertaining horror market.

As with adult novels, there are a number of options open to those who prefer to write for the YA market. Bantam still produces the Sweet Valley High and the newer Sweet Valley University series as well as the Bantam Young Adult Romance line. Two examples of the latter are *The Rumor About Julia* by Stephanie Sinclair and *A Kiss Between Friends* by Erin Haft.

The Berkley Publishing Group has a successful series called Life At Sixteen and the Splash series, Sunset Island.

Archway Books produces The Nancy Drew Series, written under a house name (many authors writing under the same name, which belongs to the publisher).

Scholastic Books publishes a series entitled Med Center. Scholastic accepts queries on YA fiction of 40,000 to 45,000 words dealing with romance, mystery and family, for readers ages twelve to fifteen who have average to good reading skills.

Books that are slanted toward specific interests are the Slasher books, a thriller genre from the Fear Street line published by Archway Books, and the popular Bantam YA fiction series by Lurlene McDaniel that explores death and dying. Most Christian book publishers, including Crossways and Bethany House Publishers, also have a line of YA novels.

Jan Mussell of Waldenbooks at Vallco Center in California says, "The most popular series for YA readers, especially boys, is the Slasher Series from Archway books. In boyfriend-girlfriend novels, the most popular lines are Sweet Valley High and Sweet Valley University. Other popular teenage romances include the love story series from Bantam, issued numerically, as well as Berkley's Sunset Island series.

"Two particularly noteworthy books about coming of age are Katherine Paterson's Newberry Award winner, *Bridge to Terabithia*, and *Jacob Have I Loved*."

First, keep in mind that YA books are written for readers who average in age from about twelve to fifteen. The protagonists in the novels usually are fifteen to eighteen, depending on the publisher's requirements. The hero and heroine are becoming more realistically complex, with interesting activities aside from dating and concerns over what to wear. They are complete with families, pets, dreams, misunderstandings and disappointments. Many of the stories deal with friendships and stress the problems concerning women's place in society.

Not all of the characters represented are the "all-American ideal." Some characters have less than admirable values, few goals in life and little interest in anything beyond themselves. The trend has caused some writers, out of a responsibility to young people, to turn down contracts from major publishers.

It is important to point out that YA novels are not adult romance novels written about younger people. When a YA heroine falls in love, she doesn't think about going to bed with the hero. She dreams about being kissed and cuddled, being taken to movies and parties and having a hamburger at McDonald's—in other words, being a couple. Unlike the heroine in the adult romance, the YA heroine doesn't often consider that the relationship will eventually lead to marriage but at that moment, being with that special boy is all important.

Where the YA novel may emphasize heartbreakingly deep emotions, the actual romance is mostly in the head of the protagonists and is realized through comparatively chaste kisses and gentle touching. Not surprisingly, the degree of sexual encounters and their intensity varies from line to line.

Teenagers love humor and if you write it well, it is a definite plus when it comes to selling your manuscript.

Kathryn Makris, author of many YA novels as well as an adaptation for television, says, "The protagonist needn't be perfect. Flaws make the characters more interesting and provide them with obstacles to overcome. Herein lies much of your plot. Stories are best when they flow from the characters. Don't squash your characters to fit your plot. Plot complexity is good but don't let plot twists and turns take precedence over your characters' growth and change."

Series novels with sets of characters who are carried over into the other books became the rage with the introduction of the Sweet Valley High books from Bantam. Since then a number of other series have been published, usually through book packagers, and have literally taken over the YA space on the bookstore shelves.

In addition to paperback novels for young adults, writers have the option of writing for the hardcover YA markets. Hardcover books are usually sold to schools or libraries and are rarely available in bookstores. Thomas Bouregy, Inc. (focusing on career, mystery, western), and Walker (focusing on mystery, suspense, western) are two such publishers. These books are less trendy than the paperbacks, have even more rigid guidelines, and have a smaller print run as well as limited distribution. As a result, the writer sees less money from the hardcover books, even though they sometimes go into paperback, limited foreign translations or large print books. Nevertheless, with hardcovers there is something uniquely satisfying about knowing that your book will be on the shelves for years instead of weeks, as happens with most series romance.

When many writers first dream of writing, they claim they would like to write for teenagers "because I don't think I have enough talent yet to write for the adult market." It is a gross misconception to think that writing for young adults is easier than writing for adults. Who, after all, is capable of understanding the teenage mind?

There are four things to consider before attempting to write in this genre.

1. You must like the genre and respect young adults.
2. You must be able to see problems and conflicts through their eyes.

3. You must have something to say that will capture their imaginations and emotions.
4. The often quoted advice, "Don't write down to your readers," should be carved in granite.

Again, quoting Kathryn Makris, "Writing Young Adult novels can be addictive. There's no time of life more rich in drama and conflict than adolescence. There are no readers more demanding of honesty than those between the ages of ten and eighteen. Add to that the sense of play and absurdity and the open-eyed freshness of adolescents, and it's hard to go back to writing for any other audience."

The most important thing a writer needs in YA writing is genuine concern for the reader—not a moralistic kind of concern, but the kind that reaches into a writer's heart for memories of what it was really like. Everyone knows how it feels to be fourteen; it's a universal experience, regardless of culture or era.

A YA novel must deal with real situations, with emotions and growth, with conflict and resolution, with characters who are believable and about whom the readers care. If there is a moral to the story, it should be woven discreetly into the fabric of plot so that a reader says, "Oh, that makes sense," instead of, "Stop with the advice already!"

If you are a writer who is intrigued by young people and flexible enough to write under strict limitations, then you may want to consider writing for the YA market. Prolific writers often find that the best part of writing for this genre is the feedback received from readers who have been touched in one way or another by the characters in the story.

Once you recognize and can write the special tone of YA novels, writing articles and stories for periodicals may be another outlet for your talents.

Writing the Inspirational or Christian Romance Novel

There is some confusion among writers as to the difference between inspirational novels and Christian novels. Inspirational novels contain an uplifting message but do not always stress the Christian influence. Christian novels are inspirational but must also contain an evangelical or Christ-based message. There is also another division, religious novels, based on non-Christian beliefs. This genre's market is growing, or at least readjusting, and there are new opportunities and certainly spiritual rewards for a writer who is able to sell to this demanding field.

For the writer who is not comfortable when writing involves sexual tension, this might be a category worth exploring. You will not be limited to contemporary inspiration. There are subcategories of historical, contemporary and mystery, as well as the same subcategories for YA inspirational and Christian novels.

Each denomination has its own doctrine. This means that your fiction must be slanted to fit those tenets. Such a simple detail as a heroine wearing jewelry or a man going to a restaurant for a steak dinner would be unacceptable in some beliefs.

Some publishers emphasize the use of biblical references and text based firmly on denominational dogma, while others stress more subtle ways of teaching Christian ideals, such as through the actions and reactions of the characters in the story. Whichever direction you choose, it is certainly necessary in this genre that you write from the heart.

Some well-known authors in the inspirational market are Phyllis Halldorson, Yvonne Lehman, Judy Baer, Donna Fletcher Crow, Jane Peart and Francine Rivers.

Bethany House publishes a wide range of fiction, including reprints of "pure" or "sweet" love stories by Grace Livingston Hill that I first read in the early forties, and a contemporary young adult series called White Dove Romances.

Yvonne Lehman has published several books for this line. They include *Picture Perfect*, dealing with teenage modeling, and *Secret Storm*, which focuses on the problems of teenagers living in an alcoholic family.

Lines come and go in the inspirational/Christian field as they do in other fields of writing. Harlequin's Steeple Hill has a line of inspirational novels called Love Inspired. While still focusing on romance, these inspirational novels deal with "men and women facing the challenge of today's world and learning important lessons about love, life and faith. Although the element of faith must be clearly present, it should be well integrated into the characterization and plot."

One of their well-published authors, Jane Peart, has published *The Risk of Loving*, which deals with acceptance and the healing power of faith at work in our daily lives.

Francine Rivers, a well-known author of romance novels, has made a name for herself as a writer for Christian book publisher Tyndale Press. *The Scarlet Thread* was on their bestseller list followed by *The*

Atonement Child. The protagonist, Dynah Carey, became pregnant after having been attacked. The conflict deals with the practical and moral decisions she must make regarding her pregnancy.

Rivers has also written a biblical novel, *Redeeming Love,* which is a five-hundred-page softcover from Multnomah Press. It is an updated story of Gomer and Hosea, set in the California gold rush period.

It is clear that writers must first understand this market before they begin to write for it, but the challenge is there. This is a growing market, and there is opportunity for those who are so inspired.

Use Romance of the Sweet Variety

Predictably, Christian romance novels deal with a love interest, but it is only a part of the story. These novels can involve a wide range of human predicaments and emotions. Care must be taken not to allow the book to become preachy; it is the quickest way to turn off an editor.

Sensuality will be a part of the book, but the sexual tension must be within acceptable bounds of kissing and embracing. Prolonged descriptions are discouraged. The hero and heroine must be able to observe certain limits of physical expression in the Christian romance.

Avoid such ploys as the "bad" person and the "good" person who brings him or her back to the church. Rediscovered faith has been overdone and is usually hard to sell. Real people facing real problems that they learn to deal with in a Christian way is the kind of story most likely to get the editor's attention.

These novels are usually written from the heroine's viewpoint in third person; however, the male's viewpoint may also be used.

Best sources of information about what is currently in demand are *Writer's Market, Novel And Short Story Writer's Market* (both from Writer's Digest Books), periodicals for writers and publishers' guidelines. Check religious bookstores as well as secular book dealers to see what is currently being published in this field.

13

How to Research Almost Anything

esearch is almost as important to the writing of a contemporary novel as it is to the writing of a historical one. The bits of information you weave into your story give it solidity and authenticity. For the contemporary novel, you will be more concerned with locales, careers, and specifics dealing with your plot. For historical novels, your research will deal with world-shaping events, costume, foods, etc.

How to Organize Research

There are several options here. Probably the best of these is electronic cataloguing, for those of you who work with computers. Database Management Systems (DBMS) enable the user to quickly enter, organize, select and access desired bits of information from a database. One might compare it to an electronic file cabinet.

With the added advantage of hypertext links on the Web, one can also access related fields with the click of a mouse. Successful research retrieval depends on how well you have your material organized. Most users have a copy of Microsoft Excel, which can be customized to fit your own data management needs. In addition to purchasing software through computer stores or catalogues, you can also download freeware or shareware database programs from the Internet.

For keeping track of deadlines, where your manuscripts are and where they have been, who owes you money, and when royalties have been paid, I recommend Swift Track. It's an excellent organizational program. For more information, write:

SwiftTrack™ For Manuscripts
14510-A Big Basin Way, Suite 125
Saratoga, CA 95070-6033

If you have yet to join the electronic parade, the tried-and-true method for keeping track of research material is the use of 3×5 file cards or legal-sized file folders. Label your cards or folders with relevant headings, such as *heroines, settings, historical research,* and so on. I use notebooks with section headings because I want room for clippings, pictures and computer printouts. I'd be the first to admit that I get more information than I have time to file, but I can usually track it down.

The important point here is to keep an accurate and up-to-date record of the source of the information: the subject, the date, the book, the author, the publisher, the information and the page where it was found. If you use more than one library (and who doesn't!), be sure to list which library had the book.

You may think you will never need the information once you've incorporated it into a manuscript, but many editors (of both contemporary and historical lines) may call and ask for a list of resources that were used. Keep in mind your research can be used over and over in future books.

There is one problem many of us face: how to know it's time to stop researching and get to work. If you love researching as much as I do, it's easy to lose track of the world around you while you're lost in some remote place in time and the universe.

A simple solution is to begin writing the book when you have the bare essentials for the locale, time period and the hook. Then, if you work on a computer, leave a series of *XXX*s where you need to embellish the background or other description. On a pad of paper, list the subjects you need to look up: food, transportation, fabrics. By waiting until later to do the research, you maintain the same narrative flow and avoid chopping up your time at the computer. It helps to do as much research as you can at one time. Don't fail to take advantage of the printers connected to automated card catalogues, they are available at many libraries. This convenience provides you with a hard copy of the source and the date you found it. Be sure to file it for future reference.

After the research is completed, it's easy enough to go back to the computer, do a global search for *XXX* and insert the material you've selected. The sources should be filed in your notebook, on file cards or in the computer for future reference. Of course, remember to record the mileage to and from the library or interviews for your tax records.

When beginning your research, the more specific you can be, the more likely you will find help. Put more simply, don't approach a subject by saying you want to learn everything you can about the War of Tripoli. The subject is too broad. Instead, begin with the date. You can find it by looking up *Tripoli* in an encyclopedia or as a keyword in the computer. This will lead you to *Tripolitan War* where you will learn the dates were 1801 to 1805. From there you can explore U.S. Naval history for those dates. You might need information about the vessels involved, the role of Stephen Decatur, the clothing of the seamen, the outcome of the decisive battle. Once you have specific questions in mind, you can browse through any number of reference books or contact the American History Library in Washington by mail or E-mail to find the answers.

The second suggestion is to become friends with reference librarians. After having used more libraries than I can remember, I have met only two or three librarians who were unwilling to help me. First, try to find the information yourself. Visit libraries during the slow hours.

Charlotte Doudell, a Cupertino, California, librarian and authority on research, gave a talk to our local romance writers' group in which she discussed several ways to research almost anything. First, concerning interviewing someone about a career or locale:

1. Be well into a project before you begin field research.
2. Do your homework first.
3. Write ahead for an appointment to the public relations contact. If interviewing on-line, make arrangements before sending a list of questions.
4. If you are going to interview someone in person, send a question list in advance of your visit. Especially if the questions are involved, this will save you time. Your interviewee will be better prepared to answer the questions.
5. Keep notes on sources. Factual information should be supported by two independent authorities. For historical details, three is better.

Learn to Use Directories

In regard to library research, Doudell recommends a check of directories. There are directories for almost any subject you want to explore: *The Official Museum Directory, Directory of Historical Societies,*

Special Library Collections Directory and even a *Directory of Directories*. There are specialized indexes, almanacs, encyclopedias, books listing reference books and bibliographies (lists of books on a particular subject). Bibliography indexes include such subjects as American history, women in literature, British history and much more. They can also suggest places to start when searching the Internet. Most libraries now have computer access, and help is available to get you started. For more information on research, see the chapter on using the Internet.

Do not overlook ordinary dictionaries. They contain much more than the definition, pronunciation and source of words. You will often find pictures of modes of transportation, flags, tools and all the little tidbits that will add flavor and authenticity to your book. Some dictionaries are specialized: dictionaries of slang, biographical dictionaries, dictionaries of classical dance and folklore, of historic events, of battles. The list is extensive.

Then there are diaries and autobiographies of famous people. You can learn everything from the style of language used at the time to the cost of a loaf of bread, to what the weather was like on a certain day.

Research for the Contemporary Novel
Researching Locations

The best way to research locations or settings is to go there. It is the one way to absorb the sounds, smells and the "feel" of a place. If you go, carry with you self-addressed manila envelopes so you can mail the material you gather to your home. This way, you aren't burdened with stacks of research booklets and brochures on a long flight home. A small tape recorder is also helpful.

If you can't go, talk to someone who has been there. Airline employees, travel agents and businesspeople who travel are usually familiar with the basic layout of an area as well as restaurants and local customs. Better yet, list your information requirements on an Internet newsgroup. Frequently someone who is a resident of the location will respond with first-hand information. I have "talked" to people from Germany, the Philippines, Mexico, Canada and Puerto Rico, to name a few. When researching an overseas locale on the Internet, use the country name as a keyword search, then further define it.

Don't forget to ask questions about the flora and fauna. Remember, don't write about trees. Write about maples, birches, hawthorns and eucalyptus. But check your information, so you don't plant birches on top of a mountain or have a flock of whooping cranes in the desert.

When all else fails, one can dig the information out of travel guides or recent books, or, if it is concerning an American locale, write to the state tourist bureau or Chamber of Commerce with a request for information. Ask for a map of the area, as well as information about points of interest. To research American geography, the New American Guide series is extremely good. There is one for every state.

At the library, check the *Directory of Newspapers*, which lists most of the newspapers published in the U.S. Then write to the circulation department and send a check for two or three dollars to pay for a copy of the Sunday edition. You can obtain information about restaurants, housing, the political and recreational scene and society in just one paper. The effort is rewarding; the information is dependable and current. Of course, most of this information is also available on the Net.

Otherwise, you can interview a travel agent, check the library reference section (both book and magazine), or write to the country's embassy in the U.S. and explain your needs. They are usually willing to help. A list of addresses can be found in *A Guide to Foreign Embassies*.

If you are really desperate, place a classified ad in a military newspaper or magazine, or a college newsletter. Chances are you will find someone who is able to answer your questions.

Researching Careers

First of all, spread the word on the Internet newsgroups and among your friends that you need to speak to a doctor (or a tree surgeon, or a scuba diver, or a chemist or a politician). It's far better to actually know an expert than to simply read about what one does. Never offer to pay interviewees, but you may take them to lunch and offer to include their name in the credits when the book is published (depending on whether your publisher will include those credits; sometimes they forget). Of course, a thank-you note after the interview is completed is mandatory. If the person was extremely helpful, it is nice to send him or her an autographed copy of the book.

Research is where networking pays off for a writer. Learn to use the Internet. Join a group such as Romance Writers of America, Mystery Writers of America or any well-organized writers club. Such organizations usually have a newsletter that has a column for writers who need help with a work in progress.

Check out the career section at the library as well as the *Readers Guide to Periodical Literature* for articles written on the subject you're researching. Another possibility would be to write nonprofit clubs or organizations of groups such as engineers, musicians and medical personnel. Sometimes the address is listed as a source in the bibliography of books on careers in that field, or the name may appear in a directory of organizations. Again, the Internet offers a wealth of resources for special interest groups. On the Internet, a Web address (URL) ending in *.org* indicates a nonprofit organization.

Research for the Historical Novel

First check the card catalogue or electronic catalogue for a specific time period and country. Then, go through selective listings such as costume, food, customs, transportation, manners, folklore, industry, entertainment, the arts, science, religion . . . any aspect of human life that would interest the reader when contrasting it against present-day life. You will probably find that each new piece of information suggests another way to expand your research. See the list of Internet addresses in chapter fourteen.

Time lines are a great resource and can be found in several sections of your library. As with all research, don't forget to explore the juvenile section. The information contained there is basic and to the point. You don't have to wade through pages of rhetoric to find the pertinent facts. Almanacs, specialized dictionaries, history books and especially chronologies are some of your best sources for time lines.

Take for example the Timetable series of books (found in the 900s in the reference section). These are a horizontal listing of who did what concurrently through the various ages of mankind. They are divided into categories: history and politics, literature and theater, religion and philosophy, visual arts and music, science and technology, and daily life. The categories are listed in columns across the top of the page. At one side, listed vertically, is a series of dates. Find the year you are looking for, then trace across to see what important events took place in each field of interest.

Let's select the year 1547. That was the year Henry VIII was succeeded by Edward VI. In the realm of theater, Henry Howard, an English poet, was executed for treason. Under Religion, La Chambre Ardente was created in France for the trial of heretics. The art world mourned the death of the Italian painter Sebastiano del Piombo about the same time that Nostradamus was making his first predictions. And Moscow was in flames.

A check of 1847 shows that all of California came under U.S. control and Liberia became an independent republic. Longfellow wrote *Evangeline* and Liszt gave his final performance. In Philadelphia, the American Medical Association was established. Babbage made known his invention of the ophthalmoscope, the first adhesive-backed postage stamps were used, and an influenza epidemic killed 15,000 people in London (from *Timetables of History*).

These are the kinds of factual tidbits we can weave into our historical fiction to help create a sense of time and place. And this is the secret to making fiction believable. There is a wealth of information available. Time lines are an exciting and effective tool that can make our work easier and more salable.

Writers can get a great deal of mileage out of research. I spent nearly a month researching the Regency period for my first Regency, but with only a small amount of additional research I was able to write seventeen more novels set in the same time period.

14

Using the Internet

*C*uriosity, as well as necessity, drives most writers to explore new alternatives to support their craft. Perhaps that's what propelled so many romance writers into the Age of the Cyberspace. And what a change it has made! Especially where research is concerned.

There are many advantages to using the Internet, which is simply a system that electronically links together computer systems all over the world by means of telephone lines.

Networking with other writers:
On-line classes
Bulletin boards
Sending/receiving mail (and with some publishers, sending your
    query letter via E-mail)
Critique groups
Marketing information
Promoting your books, classes, services
Individual home page to showcase your work

Unlimited research opportunities:
Libraries
Museums
Businesses
Publishers
Other countries
Experts in almost any field

How to Get Started on the Internet
The following is a list of what you need and what you will need to do to establish an Internet connection:

■ First you need a computer with a minimum 14,400 bps modem; 28,800 bps is faster and better because it will cost less in on-line time. Mail and other information can be read while off line. Off-line time is not charged against your account.

■ Next, you need a telephone line to hook to your computer. A separate phone line is unnecessary but handy if your computer has fax capabilities, or if you have teenagers who monopolize the telephone. A single line gives in-coming calls a busy signal when you are surfing the Internet.

■ Establish an account with a commercial on-line service such as America Online, Prodigy or Genie. Connect to one of these by calling the company's toll-free number. These companies will send you a free CD-ROM for software installation. It is a simple matter to sign on. The cost varies, but it runs about ten dollars per month for five hours of use, or twenty dollars a month for unlimited usage. Most companies offer up to fifty free hours when you first sign on.

An option to the commercial on-line services listed above are the Internet Service Providers (ISPs) such as Worldnet, Microsoft Network and Pac Bell. You should also be able to find a local ISP, which may offer a better price.

Word of warning: When signing on to a commercial provider, you will be given a list of phone numbers in your area that will connect you with on-line services. You will be asked to select one. This is the number your modem will dial each time you connect. Make very sure before you lock in your selection that the number is within your calling area, not just your area code, so there is no toll charge. Call the phone company to verify. The providers will not tell you. Failure to check this point could result in thousands of dollars in toll charges on your phone bill.

■ You will also need a credit card. Most commercial on-line services or ISPs will ask for your credit card number and will bill your card for your service on a monthly basis. Billing procedures can vary, so ask your provider for the specifics.

■ Make up a security code word or words which you should keep secret.

■ You will be asked to create an on-line code name or group of numbers for an on-line address. Mine is ptpianka@aol.com. It is fairly easy to figure out my name, but not my gender. Others prefer to use cute or funny names that do not identify their legal name.

- You do not need a printer, but most people who have computers also have printers. A printer gives you the capability to print E-mail, text and graphics, most of the information you would want to retrieve from the Internet. This feature is especially helpful when collecting research materials and important correspondence.

The cyberspace highway reaches farther than your imagination can begin to comprehend. When you open the door to the virtual world of information, you will be amazed.

Debra Mekler, president of the Silicon Valley Chapter of Romance Writers of America, is an authority on using the Internet. Here are some suggestions she has for getting started on the Internet and accessing various research sites:

"One of the best ways to begin research on the Internet is with the help of a search engine. Given a topic, the search engine (such as Yahoo) will sift through millions of Web pages for what it believes you want. Some Web sites, like search.com, allow you to find and try different engines at the same time to see what each has found. It's always a good idea to try a number of search engines. Each has its own "style," and you'll probably find one or two of preference.

"Let's assume you have accessed the Internet using a browser (such as Netscape Navigator or Microsoft Internet Explorer). At the top of your browser a horizontal box called *location* or *address* shows the address (URL) of the page you are currently viewing.

"It should be noted that Web pages have a tendency to appear and disappear with little or no warning when the individual or group owning the site decides to close down. It's best to take it in stride, as the information you want will probably be available through some other route.

"One nice thing about Web sites is page designers like to show off the other great places they have found in their own travels. These are usually identified by a *favorites* or *additional links* page. In other words, they have already done some of the legwork for you. Think of it as a springboard to further information.

"If you like a site, and want to come back to it later, set up a *bookmark*. Simply click on the button on your browser's toolbar called *bookmarks*, select *make a bookmark*. The next time you want to go to that site, select *bookmark* and choose the name of that site from your list.

"Many university libraries and their various research projects are now on-line. Countries usually have an official site approved by their government. Use the search engine to get to that country and use their pages to find other pages. You'll be amazed at the places you might end up with just a few clicks of the mouse.

"Always verify information found on the Internet through another on-line or off-line source. While there is a wealth of information at your fingertips, it's best to make sure you have the correct information."

Another way to research via the computer is through E-mail *mailing lists.* You begin by subscribing to a mailing list (also called a *list server),* usually at no cost, just by registering your name and typing in the word *subscribe.* The list is forwarded to everyone who subscribes. The open forums cover almost any subject imaginable and are participated in by a global audience. You can find out what lists are available at listserv @bitnic.cren.net, or go through an Internet search engine with a key-word (news.lists). Reference books are published listing addresses for Internet mailing lists and are available in most bookstores.

Be selective. Your mailbox will overflow. It is also important that once you receive notice stating you are a registered subscriber, print out the address and instructions on how to unsubscribe and *save them.* You will need them eventually.

Some definitions

Browser: software that allows you to go to a search engine or home-page URL.

Cyberspace: a term coined by science fiction writer William Gibson. It has become a slang term referring to both the Internet and the World Wide Web.

Download: the transfer of information from another computer to your computer. Uploading is transferring information from your computer to another computer.

E-mail: electronic mail. Enables you to send (and receive) letters, manuscripts, images . . . virtually any communication to a single subscriber or a group.

E-mail address: an Internet mailbox.

134

Hypertext/links: a connection to other sites that offer additional information on a specific subject executed with a click of the mouse.

Home page/Web page/Web site: an on-screen document used to let people know who you are, what you do. You can design the page to show text, graphics, animation, book covers and even sounds.

Internet: a system linking computers all over the world.

Newsgroups: the Internet version of a message board.

On-line: the state of your computer when it is connected "live" to another computer or computers through the use of modems and telephone lines.

Search engine: allows you to search for a specific word or phrase.

URL: Universal Resource Locator—an address for a Web site.

Publishers' URLs

Caution: remember that addresses must be copied *exactly* as shown. Address also are subject to change.

Harlequin/Silhouette: www.romance.net
Penguin USA (includes Signet, Dutton, Onyx and Topaz): www.penguin.com
Zebra: www.zebrabooks.com
Random House: www.randomhouse.com (also the site for Love Lines newsletter)
Commonwealth Publishers: www.commonwealthpub.com
Warner Books: pathfinder.com/twep
Encyclopedia Britannica Internet Guide: www.ebig.com

Bookstores

Barnes and Noble: www.barnesandnoble.com
Salon (Borders Books): www.salon.com (includes webzine with live chat capabilities)
New York Times: www.nytimes.com/books
Amazon: www.amazon.com

Writers on the Net

In a browser such as Netscape or Internet Explorer, go to one of the search engines, such as Yahoo, Excite or Infoseek. Then type in the specific subject such as writing fiction, writing science fiction, writer's help. In some search engines, quotation marks before and after the words will better pinpoint your search.

Painted Rock: www.paintedrock.com
Gothic Journal: gothicjournal.com/romance/gothshow.html

Sites of Interest

Romance Writers of America: www.rwanational.com
Jaclyn Redings—Useful Links for Romance Writers and Readers: www.inficad.com/~jacreding/romlinks.html
Library Research on the World Wide Web (with several search engines): libweb.uoregon.edu/network/srchweb.html
Index of Resources for Historians (about 2,500 connections arranged alphabetically by subject and name): kuhttp.cc.ukans.edu/history/
On-line Reference Book for Medieval Studies (written and maintained by medieval scholars for the benefit of their fellow instructors and serious students): orb.rhodes.edu/
The Labyrinth—Resources for Medieval Studies (sponsored by Georgetown University): www.georgetown.edu/labyrinth/labyrinth-home.html
Internet Modern History Sourcebook: www.fordham.edu/halsall/mod/modsbook.html
An Internet Thesaurus: www.thesaurus.com
Library of Congress: lcweb.loc.gov/
MicroReference (collection of reference sites): www.cs.uh.edu/~clifton/micro.a.html
The Awesome Library (a collection of encyclopedias): www.neat-schoolhouse.org/Library/Reference_and_Periodicals/General_Reference/Encyclopedias.html
ViVa—A Bibliography of Women's History in Historical and Women's Studies Journals: www.iisg.nl/~womhist/index.html
Researchit.Com: www.itools.com/research-it/research-it.html
The Research Paper and the World Wide Web: www.prenhall.com/~bookbind/pubbooks/rodrigues/

Note: If you are given a URL from a source such as E-mail and would like to go to that site . . . the easiest way to copy the URL is to highlight it, go to *Edit*, click on *Copy*, then go to the browser and put the cursor on the location bar. Go to *Edit*, click on *Paste*, and the URL will appear in the location bar. Then hit *Enter* and it should take you to the site. It saves the time and effort of trying to copy a long URL. Then if the site proves helpful, be sure to make a bookmark for easy return.

How to Submit Your Manuscript to a Publisher

15

The submission of a carefully prepared manuscript with a minimum of typos not only makes the work easier for an editor, but it is a measure of the quality of your work. Instructions on how to set up and submit a manuscript can be found in *Writer's Digest Guide to Manuscript Formats* by Buchman and Groves (Writer's Digest Books). If you wish to submit first to an agent, you might consult Michael Larsen's, *Literary Agents: What They Do, How They Do It, and How to Find and Work With the Right One for You* (John Wiley & Sons, Inc.).

Beginning writers are usually asked to first submit a query before sending an in-depth synopsis or completed manuscript. Consult the guidelines or *Writer's Market* (an annual book from Writer's Digest Books, considered the authority on marketing manuscripts) before sending a finished manuscript.

Remember that your query and synopsis are your sales pitch to an editor. The proposal should demonstrate your best writing ability.

Note: At one time, editors wanted synopses single-spaced because they did not edit between lines. The trend has changed. Most editors now prefer double-spaced synopses. A ragged right margin is preferred instead of a justified right margin.

What Makes a Good Query Letter?

If you are submitting a romance short story or novella, it is unnecessary to query first. Do, however, send a cover letter listing your credentials with your story. When proposing a novel to a publisher or agent, a query letter is, almost without exception, a necessity.

A query letter is an encapsulated version (one or two pages) of the story you are trying to propose. It is single spaced in the usual business letter format.

The letter should include a short summary of your book, your credits, pertinent affiliations and your authority for writing the book (degree in history, extensive research, the many books you have read in this category). You may also include one-paragraph character sketches on a separate sheet of paper. Keep the query short, tight, fast moving, informative, and include your phone number. A sample query letter follows on page 140.

A query letter may be up to three pages long. The basic elements to include are:

1. A short but interesting sketch of your novel.
2. A few words about which line you slanted the book toward.
3. A paragraph listing your credits. If you have no publishing credits, say you are a freelance writer, then state your interest in the subject and your research and affiliations as your authority for writing the book.
4. The final paragraph should be your offer to send additional material if the editor would like to see it.

Thank the editor and mention that a SASE is enclosed. If you are writing to a foreign publisher, enclose IRCs (International Reply Coupons, which can be purchased at larger post offices).

Note: When writing to Harlequin or Silhouette or another publishing house which has several lines, it helps to write on the front, left, bottom corner of your envelope, "Query: Harlequin Intrigue (or the appropriate line)." The reason is that the lines arc shuffled around and the editor may have been reassigned. Being specific saves time.

The Synopsis

The word *synopsis* is often incorrectly used interchangeably with the word *outline*. An *outline* is a detailed, chapter-by-chapter breakdown listing the areas of importance, as opposed to a narration. The outline, along with a table of contents and sample chapters, is used for the nonfiction book proposal.

A *synopsis* might be compared to a short story without dialogue. It is a summary in narrative form of the text of a fictional work. It should accomplish three basic functions: state the premise of your novel,

Dear (editor's name):

Midsummer Madness is the story of two people who risk their lives to prove that corrupt city officials are involved in a cover-up that has already killed innocent people and threatens to destroy a town. It is a Romantic Intrigue that I would like you to consider for publication in (name the line).

Janina Scott was experienced enough as a nurse to know that something was dreadfully wrong at the Northern California hospital where she is employed as Patient Advocate. There had to be some explanation for the sudden increase in pancreatitis cases but no one in a position of authority would listen to her.

As the book opens, David Madison, on sabbatical from his San Diego hospital, reenters her life and wants to marry her. Janina had been seriously involved with the handsome surgeon when he suddenly married his childhood sweetheart. In the ensuing two years, Janina tried unsuccessfully to overcome her infatuation for him by devoting her energies to her work and to her family. Recently, her younger sister, Debbie, has been running around with a wild crowd and Janina is concerned.

As the story progresses, David and Janina join forces to investigate the possibility that malathion, an aerial spray used to combat fruit flies, is the cause of the pancreatitis census. They are chased by security police, make a commando raid on a helicopter refueling site, and take on City Hall in a dramatic move to uncover the cover-up. The story includes elements of humor, some sensual love scenes, and a number of twists and turns as well as a tension-filled ending where Janina and David win out over City Hall.

I am an avid reader of (name the line). My writing credits include: (if you have published, name title, date and publisher). I am actively involved with a writing critique group (or RWA or other organization). (Include other credits which make you an authority on something involved in the book, or mention your extensive research if you have no recognized credit, such as a degree in history or medicine.)

If the premise of the book appeals to you I can send an in-depth synopsis and the first three chapters. Thank you for your time and interest in my work. SASE (or IRC) enclosed.

(Close with "Sincerely," and sign your name.)

Sample Query Letter

delineate and show motivation for the main characters, and detail the significant stages of plot development.

The Advantages of Writing a Synopsis

The synopsis tells the editor what kind of a book you are writing and what the book is about. The way you handle your synopsis demonstrates your creative ability to capsulize a plot, to handle the natural progression of a story and to hook the reader within a limited number of pages.

There are other advantages for the author who writes the synopsis *before writing the book*. It is easier to write the synopsis first. Once the book is written, you will have created such a wealth of great scenes that it will be difficult to choose those that are the most significant to the momentum of the story.

A well-written synopsis will let you know at a glance if you have enough plot to fill the required number of pages. It can be broken down into an outline in which you can count the number of scenes per chapter. You will be able to judge whether the action is well paced and if the major scenes generate new scenes and lead into the next chapter. You will be able to tell if your characters are well developed and whether they stay within character.

For a first-time author, the chances are remote that an editor will offer a contract on the basis of a synopsis and sample chapters, but from the editor's comments you will at least know if you are headed in the right direction. There may be certain aspects of the novel that your editor will want changed. It is much less frustrating to do this before you have written an entire book than after the manuscript has been completed.

Once you have established a track record, most editors will offer a contract on the basis of a synopsis or a synopsis and sample chapters. There is nothing like a signed contract to motivate you to sit at the typewriter.

How to Write a Synopsis

Beginning writers always ask how long a synopsis should be. It is difficult to answer this question because there are so many variables. Some editors specify in the guidelines that they will read only a one-page synopsis or query letter. It is difficult to condense all the information contained in 60,000 words into one page. If the query letter interests them, they will probably ask for an in-depth synopsis.

For a novel of 50,000 to 75,000 words, a synopsis might run to six double-spaced pages. It is usually wise to try to limit the synopsis to ten pages. Of course if the plot is extremely intricate, it could require more space to explain the fine details. If the synopsis is of a single title novel of 100,000 words or more, the synopsis could be much longer. There is no precise rule, but avoid wordiness.

The Eleven Basic Elements of the Synopsis

A synopsis of a novel should contribute in narrative form the same ingredients that make up a novel. The eleven components may be used in a different sequence but none may be omitted.

1. Setting: One of the first paragraphs should give the editor the time period and the geographical location of your novel—the arena of action.

2. The main characters: The heroine and hero should be introduced as early as possible. In the case of a single viewpoint character as in a few series novels, it usually works best to begin the synopsis with the viewpoint character. Although it is not necessary to introduce into the synopsis all the characters in your novel, it is important to name those who play influential roles in the development of the plot. Each main character should have a goal!

3. The family background: This should be brought into the synopsis at this time. It may not enter into the book in its entirety, but it enables both the writer and the editor to understand motivation. This tells the *why* of the plot. Why the characters are where they are at a given time.

4. The critical situation: This should also begin to develop at about the same time as the portrayal of the main characters. The critical situation is the dramatic change that has just taken place or is about to take place—a change that will affect the characters for the rest of their lives. It sets up the conflict.

5. Mood: Introspection is used in the synopsis to show characterization and motivation and to set the tone of the book. Dialogue is rarely used in a synopsis, but introspection is a valuable tool.

6. Conflict: Drama is born out of conflict. Be sure to stress the conflict in your synopsis. It is the substance of your novel and usually arises out of the critical situation and the character's goals, wants, needs.

The foregoing elements, with the possible exception of some of the characters, will usually appear in the first chapter of your novel. Once you have the foundation, you can go on to the key scenes.

7. Key scenes: A novel usually has three scenes per chapter and a big scene every fifth chapter. It is impossible and unwise to depict every scene in the synopsis, but do make it a point to emphasize the important scenes: those that show deep emotion, a change in the character of the protagonist, and movement in the story. Next to believable characters, these are what sell your novel.

8. Advance and retreat: The accomplishment of goals should never be made easy for our protagonist. It is the struggle that makes success so sweet in the end. The setbacks add substance to the story, so be sure to include some of them in your synopsis.

9. Turn-around scene: The "come to realize" scene is a pivotal scene where the protagonist gains insight into her feelings or the events that have occurred. Decisions made at this time can either hinder or advance her goals depending on whether she makes the right decision or the wrong one.

10. Climax: The crucial final scene where the protagonist achieves her goal is an important part of the synopsis. Don't make the editor guess how the book ends. If the synopsis is well written enough to capture her interest, you can be sure she will want to read the book—even though she knows how it ends.

11. The conclusion: This is the easy let-down from the action and tension of the conflict. It is the satisfying ending where all the loose ends are tied up and the characters find the happiness and contentment they have been searching for. Romance novels always have a happy ending.

A Few Hints

If you need to explain specific scenes or motivation, simply enclose the explanation in parentheses at the appropriate place in the synopsis.

Most synopses are written in present tense, with the back story (background information) written in past tense.

A Checklist for the Synopsis

1. Does the beginning of the synopsis establish the viewpoint and secondary characters?
2. Does it inform the reader as to geographical setting, time period and mood of the story: humorous, romantic, serious, etc.?

3. Does the synopsis show enough movement or action leading to the conclusion?
4. Is the action well paced?
5. Do you plant clues, and if so, do you follow up on them?
6. Does each scene leave the reader in anticipation of the next scene?
7. Is each scene necessary to the story? Few things antagonize an editor or reader more than words used simply to fill space.
8. Do you follow through on your critical situation and bring it to a logical conclusion?
9. Do you make full use of characterization techniques? Do you show motivation?
10. Is your final manuscript edited and typed to the best of your ability? You are competing with professionals. Let the appearance of your copy be one more point in your favor.
11. Are you sending it to the best possible market? Poor marketing can ruin a sale as easily as poor writing.

Added Incentives

Along with a synopsis, sample chapters and cover letter, many authors include a page or two of character sketches. If your characters are well drawn, further information about them can increase the salability of your manuscript as well as providing book cover information. This is also the best way to make certain that the cover models match your characters' physical descriptions.

Character Sketch for *Midsummer Madness*
by
Phyllis Taylor Pianka

Janina Scott: has lived most of her life in the San Francisco Bay area of Northern California where she earned her degree in nursing. After working for several years in emergency she found she was unable to distance herself from the pain and suffering. Fearing burnout, she became a Patient Advocate, a job well suited to her belief that the patient's welfare must be considered first. Work is her cure for the loneliness which began when David Madison, whom she had hoped to marry, suddenly left her to wed his childhood sweetheart. She has since dated other men but they always fell short of her expectations. Despite this emptiness in her life, Janina finds contentment in her work, through an occasional visit with her family; the company of Cinnamon, her pet cat; and through working with potted plants which fill her house and patio. Description: 5′8″ tall; golden brown, just-above-the-shoulder hair; fair skin; blue eyes.

David Madison: is the kind of man most women would like to fall in love with. If he has one flaw, it's his determination to do the right thing, no matter what it might cost him emotionally. The hardest decision of his life was when he left Janina to marry his childhood sweetheart who was dying and needed someone to look after her. He cared deeply for this woman who was wife in name only, but it couldn't begin to compare with the love he had for Janina. He counted on the strength of that love to see them through until the time would come, inevitably, when he would be free to ask her to marry him. Now that his wife is gone he plans to use a part of his inheritance to set up a clinic for preventive medicine for the underprivileged in San Diego. Description: 6′2″ tall; dark hair; sun-tanned complexion from playing tennis; lean physique; long, slender, capable hands.

Debbie Scott: Janina's kid sister. Basically a nice girl but at present she is undecided what she wants to do with her life. She is in love with Doug but is impatient with the competition she feels between her and his training to be a doctor. She drifts into a friendship with an undisciplined crowd and begins dating one of the less-than-savory characters. Her relationship with her parents is much the same as Janina's—the ties are close but there is little in common except their relationship. As a show of independence, Debbie starts drinking, a situation that brings about a confrontation between her and her mother. Janina is called in as a peacemaker.

Doug Fairfax: Medical student, also holding down a job in patient care at a nursing home in order to help put himself through school. His father owns a small air-conditioning service company. Doug and his father are close, even though they see each other rarely because of Doug's schedule. Doug could be considered a younger version of David. Although his first allegiance lies with his medical training, his pursuit of Debbie runs a close second.

Synopsis for *Midsummer Madness*

by

Phyllis Taylor Pianka

Janina Scott is serious about her job as Patient Advocate at Mercy Community Hospital in Willowbrook, California. When an unusual number of people are admitted to intensive care with symptoms of acute pancreatitis, she starts checking the records and finds that a single thread of evidence draws them together. All of the patients reside in the foothills, an area just outside the small Northern California town. Unfortunately, some pieces to the puzzle are missing.

About this time David Madison reenters her life. They had been dating quite regularly for a while when David broke it off and married his high school sweetheart. She was dying and needed someone to take care of her, but Janina always wondered if it was his wife's money that attracted David.

Janina had never quite gotten over him. She is determined to go slow before reopening that particular door and becoming involved in a serious relationship with David, now a doctor on a month's sabbatical from a San Diego hospital.

At first David thinks Janina is borrowing trouble when she questions the sudden increase in hemorrhagic pancreatitis, but when she talks him into going with her to City Hall to check with the zoning department to see if there is a central source of the infection, they discover that a secret emergency meeting is being held. They are unable to learn anything more and are practically ejected from the building.

Careful investigation reveals that a more intensive spray program is being undertaken, ostensibly to combat a sudden invasion of the fruit fly which could threaten the lush farming valley. Local residents have long complained that the chemical formula used in the aerial spray programs is the cause of all manner of respiratory and other serious infections. David assures Janina that the spray is perfectly safe because it has been used for a long period of time in various communities across the country.

But when Janina insists, David takes her to the Langtree Laboratory Experimental Station in the foothills. When they try to get in to question someone about the use of the chemical spray, they find that new barricades have been erected and extreme security precautions are being enforced. They are unable to get in, and when they ask to talk to the director, he is unavailable.

Instinct tells Janina that something is dreadfully wrong. She used to date a man who once worked at the Experimental Station, and she had been inside the grounds and buildings many times. The new emphasis on security is both unbelievable and puzzling.

All roads surrounding the facility have been blocked off and there is no way, short of walking, that they can go around the property to inspect it from the outside. The next day is Janina's day off. David suggests they take a picnic and rent horses from a nearby stable. Janina is aware of the fact that he is not fully convinced that something is being covered up, and she knows that he is trying to humor her by renting horses so they can get a closer look at the station grounds.

His consideration of her feelings rekindles the warm feelings she had for David and she finds herself thinking of him in a romantic way. Despite her anxiety to survey the perimeter of the buildings, they have a lovely picnic in an isolated woodsy glen. David holds her in his arms and they kiss and talk about the past.

But when they ride around the newly installed chain link fence, they can see in the distance men clothed in heavy suits and masks, intensively spraying the ground and outside of a building that houses the new products lab. Just as they are about to get a closer look, a pair of motorcycle police approach them with weapons drawn. Janina and David are forced to identify themselves and they are warned that if they are seen in the area again they will be arrested.

David is now convinced that Janina's suspicions are not without foundation. When they try to talk to the city manager they are at first accused of overactive imaginations, then are warned in no uncertain terms not to start something that could result in a great deal of trouble for them and the community.

Janina tries to argue that the community is already involved, that people are near death in the intensive care unit at the hospital. She tells him that the Langtree Company must be spraying chemicals that cause the infections. The official reminds her that Langtree makes chemicals only for medical applications, not agricultural sprays. She knows he's telling the truth.

For the next week Janina's concern over her sister, Debbie, who has gotten involved with a rough group of characters, takes up most of her thoughts. She would prefer that Debbie resume her relationship with Doug Fairfax, son of the owner of a small industrial air-conditioning company. Doug, who is studying to be a doctor, works part time in a convalescent home to help pay for his tuition.

Then, too, Janina has been seeing more of David and they have resumed a guarded relationship. David wants to make love to her but at first he insists on courting her to make up for all the years they spent apart. Janina is touched. There is no doubt in her mind that she still loves him. The question is, can she trust him this time?

One night they go for a drive in the country, ending up in the foothills near the laboratory. Suddenly they realize they have been followed for the last ten minutes. David pulls into a grove of trees and a police car creeps on by.

Meanwhile, in town, the local Department of Agriculture announces a stepped-up aerial spray campaign to eradicate the fruit fly that they claim threatens to destroy the local peach and apricot crops. To confirm their suspicions, David and Janina visit several of the larger growers and inquire about conditions. No one reports having seen any fruit flies, but they are all in favor of the massive spray campaigns, which they assume are protecting them.

That night they find out where the staging ground is for the helicopters involved in the aerial spray, and they manage to get a sample of the chemical being used. Analysis proves that it is not the malathion, which was the chemical they were said to have used, but a more toxic spray used to control certain virulent forms of bacteria.

David and Janina try to get a local reporter to help them in their investigation and he agrees. Later they find that the editor refused to print such "alarmist" stories.

Janina now has to admit what she feared is true. Willowbrook is a company town. Most of the businesses and residents rely on the various Langtree industries to support them.

In her frustration over their inability to uncover the truth, Janina causes trouble at the hospital and is asked to take a few days off to get herself under control.

That night Doug's father is admitted to the hospital in an advanced stage of hemorrhagic pancreatitis. Doug reveals that his father has been installing new air-conditioning filters at the medical lab in the foothills.

Debbie is there when they question Doug. In an effort to comfort Doug, she goes for a ride with him to the beach in his dad's new truck. Debbie really likes him, but his work and schooling keep Doug so busy he has had little time for her.

That night Debbie is admitted to the hospital with preliminary symptoms of pancreatitis. It puzzles them that Doug shows no ill effects until they finally put together the pieces and figure out that those people who have been given gamma globulin shots are immune to what they are now convinced is a mutant bacteria. Doug, in his capacity as an orderly, had been given the medicine as protection against the infectious hepatitis, which had gotten a foothold in the convalescent home.

Janina blames herself for not doing more to protect her sister. In her anxiety, Janina turns to David for comfort and they make love. He stays with her from then on and they find in each other all the splendor of a love too long denied. (Nice warm, gentle, sensual love scenes here.)

Debbie's condition remains stable. Doug spends a great deal of time with her and they reach an understanding of sorts.

In the meantime, the hospital administrator, who was firmly entrenched in city politics, is unwilling to give any more time to Janina and David. They decide the only way to get the city's attention is to confront the board members at the next council meeting.

Janina and David make it appear they have broken into the Langtree lab and when the city council convenes, Janina and David pretend to have in their possession a canister of the bacterial spores that they deduce are the airborne source of the infections. There is panic in City Hall but David has locked the doors to prevent anyone from leaving or entering.

Confronted with the evidence, the city manager finally admits the truth. The laboratory has been experimenting with a newly discovered mutant form of bacteria, which has proved more virulent than they ever imagined. It had accidentally gotten into the air-conditioning system and had escaped into a small area of the surrounding neighborhood. The massive fruit fly spraying program was merely a cover-up to enable them to spray for the bacteria without alarming the local residents.

Doug's father received a more potent dose because at the time he replaced the defective filters, they were not aware of the source of the leak.

Contamination had gotten into the truck from Doug's father's clothing and when Doug and Debbie went to the beach, Debbie was infected by the bacteria.

The city officials are still unwilling to force a confrontation with the owners of Langtree Labs because they are afraid of the effect it will have on the city. But David and Janina tell them it's too late. The meeting of the council has been televised by the local cable TV station and the film has already been removed to a safe place for future broadcast in the event the council fails to cooperate. The officials capitulate.

The laboratory is subsequently ordered to confine its experiments to the testing of medical products, as they had in the past, and to make a settlement to anyone who had suffered ill effects from the bacteria. Debbie, along with most of the other patients, recovers from her illness after receiving massive doses of gamma globulin. Debbie is properly grateful to Doug for his extreme concern during her illness. And David and Janina marry and move to San Diego where he again takes up his medical practice. The end.

16
Avoiding the Pitfalls

The dictionary defines a pitfall as an unexpected trap. Advance knowledge is the best prevention against failure, yet we must be mature enough to recognize that some pitfalls are unavoidable. We can't always foresee editorial changes or subject duplication.

Some of the things to avoid, according to an editor's panel at the national Romance Writers of America Conference, are stories involving the theater, ballet, the fine arts, sports, computer careers, jealousy, more than one male love interest, long chunks of background information, and withheld information.

Leslie Wainger, Senior Editor and Editorial Coordinator at Silhouette Books, in talking about elements of mystery, says that she isn't looking for parallel plots, like two trains running on opposite tracks, "then stopping and one invites the other to dinner." The mystery must affect the relationship. The protagonists must solve the mystery together. The mystery could be a starting point or come in later, but it must be an integral part of the romance. Wainger shared that Silhouette tries not to give "do's and don'ts" because the success of a book is how it's handled.

"It's very easy to write down to an audience," Wainger said, "relying on strings of adjectives, flowery dialogue, immature characters, and all-too-familiar plots to get from page one to page two hundred and one, but readers can't be fooled by this approach anymore—if they ever could be!"

Kathryn Falk, publisher of *Romantic Times*, said, "Writing the romance today is much different than it was in the early 1980s when

I started *Romantic Times* and wrote *Love's Leading Ladies* and *How to Write a Romance and Get It Published.*

"The industry has changed and developed, and whereas there was little information for the aspiring writer at the beginning, now there are books, conferences, writing groups and cassette tapes.

"Certain principles apply today. A new writer should try hard to create something fresh and different from what has preceded. That means a writer must be familiar with the genre she is writing in and try to write the 'next' evolvement of something that takes it one step farther.

"I suggest that a new writer, after reading all the best of the genre, should ask herself, what can I do to add something new to what exists?"

Louise Snead, of *Affaire de Coeur*, an internationally circulated magazine for romance readers and writers, said, "If you talk to the people in the industry, they will sum up the outlook for romance writers in two words . . . 'not good.' The reasons for this conclusion are numerous:

- The market has been flooded with romances.
- The quality of romances has plummeted.
- The cost of a single title makes a buyer more careful and selective in his/her purchase.
- From the writer's perspective, the advances are low, and the royalties may be few and far between.
- It is a publisher's market—if you don't like their proposal, there are a thousand people waiting to accept it.

"Does 'not good' mean impossible? Not at all. New writers can still enter the market and do well with a career in writing. But that writer has to be smart.

"First and foremost, write a darn good book. No reader complains when they buy a book and it's good. It's the poorly written fare with overworked plots and stereotypical characterizations that earn the disdain of readers. Far too many writers fall into the trap of quantity versus quality. That is, they will publish two to three or more books, and those books are substandard. It doesn't take long for the reader to dismiss that writer as mediocre.

"Secondly, let someone know your book is out there. In other words, *market your work.* An author cannot depend upon word of mouth for the sales of her books. When it comes to the business aspect of writing, many authors like to bury their heads in the sand. What is the point in creating a product if no one knows it's there? If you're proud of what you've done, if that work is good, then let people know about it. Get it reviewed by as many publications as you can. Do book signings whenever possible. Take out ads. Nothing is sadder than reading a book by an author no one has ever heard of and learning that author has two to three previously released books.

"There are many publications that will not review your work. Support the ones who do. Remember, they get more novels for review than they can possibly use. When they select yours, they are doing you a favor in helping to get your novel in the public eye. Do your homework and find out their deadline dates. Be courteous. A thank-you goes a long way.

"The outlook for the romance writer is directly related to that writer's perseverance, talent and energy. Write a good book and help sell it. If you do, you'll beat the odds and reap the rewards."

A word of encouragement from Silhouette editor Leslie Wainger: "I think authors, both the old-timers and the aspiring newcomers, need to be reminded that what they may see as a shrinking market is, in many ways, a growing one. Not only are specific lines doing better all the time, but when readers have fewer books to choose from, their purchases are concentrated on those titles that remain, making for a higher per-title sell-through. And a new author, a new voice, is always welcomed eagerly by editors and readers alike. I firmly believe that a good book will always find a home, and a look at the number of new authors appearing in the various Silhouette Books lines all the time provides confirmation of that fact.

"In the end, we're all trying to satisfy the reading public. The editor's desk is merely a way station on that journey, not the end of the trip."

Journeys. Even the word sounds as if it has been drawn from some magic elixir and distilled through the gossamer screen of the imagination.

As I sit here in my studio and read again the quotation pinned to my bulletin board, "A journey of a thousand miles begins with a single step," I wonder how many writers will begin today to take that first step. I remember my own beginning and the indescribable joy of receiving my first contract. I wish the same thing for you. May you find the road map I've provided a help in avoiding the potholes along the way, and a sure and certain guide to the points of interest, the treasures that are there for the seeking at every turn of the page.

53 Reasons Why a Book May Be Rejected

1. Failure to probe the depths of your characters.
2. Characters failed to stay within character.
3. Characters were clichéd or unbelievable.
4. Characters were unsympathetic.
5. Secondary male outshone the hero.
6. There were too many characters (or too few).
7. The characters were confusing/not clearly drawn.
8. There was inadequate contrast between characters.
9. Incorrect balance between dialogue and narration.
10. Dialogue was not believable.
11. Characters and dialogue lacked sparkle.
12. Profanity not acceptable. Or, overuse of slang words.
13. Plot or characters lacked substance.
14. Not enough conflict to support a book of this length.
15. The conflict was not believable.
16. The conflict began too far from the opening.
17. There was no opening hook—no critical situation.
18. The opening was too slow. Book opened too soon.
19. The novel was not cohesive.
20. There was nothing to hang the book on/no premise.
21. Too much/not enough action.
22. The writing (plot) was too fragmented.
23. The setting was not important enough.
24. Too much emphasis placed on the setting.
25. The setting has been overused.
26. Author has failed to research the setting.
27. Too much or not enough background information.
28. Too little background of characters.
29. Too much or not enough sensuality.
30. The book was overwritten.
31. The manuscript was sent to the wrong market.
32. The publisher is currently overstocked.
33. The publisher is not currently publishing novels of this category.

34. Too many subplots or not enough subplots.
35. The plot is too familiar.
36. The plot is too thin. Not enough conflict for the length.
37. The plot is inappropriate to this category.
38. The plot moves too quickly or too slowly.
39. The author has left out mandatory scenes.
40. Some scenes were rushed. Some scenes were too long.
41. There were not enough scenes per chapter.
42. The transitions were not sufficient to show time changes.
43. The length does not fit the category or publisher's needs.
44. The novel was poorly researched.
45. This period in history is not salable.
46. Too much emphasis on history, too little on characters.
47. The book was too preachy.
48. The book sagged in the middle. Poor pacing.
49. There is no reader identification with characters.
50. The writing is out of context for the age of the publisher's readership.
51. Too many loose ends were left dangling.
52. The story lacks drama/emotion.
53. Poor manuscript preparation.

Appendix
Reference Sources

Note: Some of these references are out of print or unavailable for purchase, but you should be able to find them in your local library.

The Art of Compelling Fiction, Christopher T. Leland. Cincinnati: Story Press, 1998.

Beginning Writer's Answer Book, ed. Kirk Polking. Cincinnati: Writer's Digest Books, 1994.

The Elements of Style, William Strunk. New York: Macmillan, 1979.

Handbook of Short Story Writing, Vol. I & II, Dix/Smythe/Fredette. Cincinnati: Writer's Digest Books, 1991.

Literary Agents: What They Do, How They Do It, and How to Find and Work With the Right One for You, Michael Larsen. New York: John Wiley & Sons, Inc., 1996.

Literary Market Place, New York: R. R. Bowker., updated annually. Annual marketing guide for writers.

The Writer's Digest Guide to Manuscript Formats, Dian Dincin Buchman and Seli Groves. Cincinnati: Writer's Digest Books, 1988.

Writer's Market, Cincinnati: Writer's Digest Books, updated annually. Annual directory featuring over 4,000 markets for writers.

The Writer's Journey: Mythic Structure for Storytellers and Screenwriters, Christopher Vogler. Studio City, CA: Michael Wiese Productions, 1992.

Writing Romances: A Handbook by the Romance Writers of America, ed. Rita Gallagher and Rita Clay Estrada. Cincinnati: Writer's Digest Books, 1997.

Library Reference Books
For Dialogue:

An Actor's Encyclopedia of Dialects, Donald Molin. New York: Sterling Publishers, 1984.

American Tramp and Underworld Slang, Godfrey Irwin. New York: Gale Research, 1971.

Black English, Joey Lee Dillard. San Francisco: Seabury Press (Harper Religious Books), 1977.

The Concise Dictionary of Twenty-Six Languages in Simultaneous Translation, Peter Bergman. Fairfax, VA: Polyglot Library, 1968.

Cowboy Slang, Edgar Frosty Potter. Phoenix: Golden West Publishers, 1986.

A Dictionary of Slang and Unconventional English, Eric Partridge. New York: Macmillan Publishers, 1985.

Indian Talk, Iron Eyes Cody. Happy Camp, CA: Naturegraph Company, 1970.

Slang—Today and Yesterday, Eric Partridge. New York: Bonanza Books (Crown Publishers), 1970.

Talkin' and Testifyin', Geneva Smitherman. Boston: Houghton Mifflin, 1977.

For Characterization:

American Given Names, George R. Stewart. New York: Oxford University Press, 1979.

The Art of Dramatic Writing, Lajos Egri. New York: Simon Schuster, 1977.

Characterization and Viewpoint, Orson Scott Card. Cincinnati: Writer's Digest Books, 1988.

Characters Make Your Story, Maren Elwood. Boston: The Writer, Inc., 1987.

Fiction Is Folks, Robert Newton Peck. Cincinnati: Writer's Digest Books, 1982.

How to Write Best-Selling Fiction, Dean Koontz. Cincinnati: Writer's Digest Books, 1981.

Professional Fiction Writing, Jean Owen. Boston: The Writer, Inc., 1974.

For Regency Period:

The Best Behavior, Esther B. Aresty. New York: Simon & Schuster, 1970. (antique etiquette)

Coaching Days/Coaching Ways, W. Outram Tristram. London: Bracken Books, 1985. (includes pencil sketches, good travel and entertainment information)

A Collector's History of Fans, Nancy Armstrong. New York: Clarkson N. Potter Publisher (Crown), 1974.

English Costumes of the 19th Century, James Laver. New York: Hawthorn Books, 1964.

English Cottages and Farmhouses, Olive Cook. New York: Thames and Hudson Publishers, 1982.

English Country House, Gervase Jackson-Stops. New York: Little, Brown and Company, 1982.

The English Country House and Its Furnishings, Michael Wilson. Stamford, CT: Architectural Book Publishing Company, 1978.

Fashions from Ancient Egypt to the Present Day, Mila Contini. Indianapolis: Oddyssey Press, 1963.

The Folklore of the Sea, Margaret Bakel. London: David and Charles Publishers, 1979.

Illustrated English Social History, Vol. 4, George Macauly Trevelyan. New York: McKay (Random House), 1978.

Leisure and Pleasure in the 18th Century, Stella Margetson. Cassell, 1971.

Leisure and Pleasure in the 19th Century, Stella Margetson. New York: Coward & McCann, 1969.

Life in Regency England, R. J. White. New York: G. P. Putnam's Sons, 1963.

London, a Concise History, Geoffrey Trease. New York: Charles Scribner's Sons, 1975.

Love and the Princesses, Lucille Iremonger. New York: Crowell Publishers (Macmillan), 1960.

Marlborough House Set, Anita Leslie. New York: Doubleday, 1972.

Mrs. Hurst Dancing (1812-1823), Gordon Mingay. London: Victor Gollancz Ltd., 1981.

The Prince of Pleasure and His Regency, J.B. Priestly. New York: Harper, 1969.

Private Palaces: Life in the Great London Houses, Christopher Simon Sykes. New York: Viking, 1986.

Regency London, Stella Margetson. Praeger Publishers, 1971.

The Rise and Fall of the Regency Dandy, T.A.J. Bumett. Boston: Little, Brown and Company, 1981. (The life and times of Berdmore Davies)

Royal Palaces, Phillip Howard. Boston: Gambit, Inc., 1970.

Writer's Guide to Everyday Life in the 1800s, Marc McCutcheon. Cincinnati: Writer's Digest Books, 1993.

Writer's Guide to Everyday Life in Regency and Victorian England, Kristine Hughes. Cincinnati: Writer's Digest Books, 1998.

Periodicals: Newsstands or by Subscription

Publishers Weekly
245 W. 17th St.
New York, NY 10011

The Writer
120 Boylston Street
Boston, MA 02116-4615
Web site: www.channel1.com/the writer/

Writer's Digest
1507 Dana Ave.
Cincinnati, OH 45207

Romance Industry Trade Periodicals

Affaire de Coeur
Louise Snead, editor
3976 Oak Hill Rd.
Oakland, CA 94605

(510) 596-5675 Fax: (510) 632-8868
E-mail: sseven@msn.com

Manderley
P.O. Box 679
Boonville, CA 95415
(707) 895-3822
(free catalogue with reviews)

Rawhide and Lace
P.O. Box 11593
Bainbridge Island, WA 98110

The Regency Plume
711 D. Street Northwest
Ardmore, OK 73401

Rendezvous
1507 Burnham Ave.
Calumet City, IL 60409
(708) 291-8337
(reviews and market news)

The Romantic Times
55 Bergen Street
Brooklyn, NY 11201

Romance Writer's Report
Romance Writers of America
13700 Veterans Memorial Drive, Suite 315
Houston, TX 77014
(713) 440-6885

Index